Rocky Wildflowers

Field Guide

Revised and Expanded Second Edition

by Linda S. Nagy

with photographs by Bernie Nagy

"To see a World in a Grain of Sand,
and a Heaven in a Wild Flower..."

-William Blake

Credits and Acknowledgements:

Author: Linda S. Nagy

Photography, Page and Cover Design: Bernie Nagy

Illustrations and Print-ready Production: Linda Nagy

Editors & Botanical Reviews: Bernie Nagy, Mariska Hamstra, Al Schneider, and Keith & Vivian Pershing

Copyright: 2013, 2014, 2015, 2016

High Country Artworks, LLC

Published and distributed by:

High Country Artworks, LLC
PO Box 1795, Fairplay, CO 80440
www.highcountryartworks.com
email: info@highcountryartworks.com

ISBN: 978-0-9840636-7-3

Library of Congress Control Number: 2015905569

Second Edition, First Printing 2016
Printed in Korea

This field guide is dedicated to all wildflower lovers in the High Country and to our beloved granddaughter, Amari, a nature lover and budding artist.

Dear Wildflower Enthusiast,

Nature lovers and those who hike throughout the Southern Rockies of Colorado and the Central Rockies of Wyoming will enjoy this little book while learning more about wildflowers. Each wildflower included has its own page with photos, names, and a description. Common names are listed first in large type and alternate names are shown in parentheses.

One should be aware that common names vary from person to person and from region to region. Many flowers have several common names and others have no common names; but all have scientific names.

Scientific names are standard all over the world and allow everyone to speak the same language. In this wildflower book, the scientific name is listed in italics followed by a synonym. Next, the common family name of the wildflower species and its scientific name are listed. Scientific names are taken from John Kartez's, the Biota of North America Program (www.bonap.org) with synonyms by Colorado plant authority, William A. Weber. Traditional family names are given along with new family classifications recommended by the **Angiosperm Phylogency Group** in 2009 **(APG III).**

Wildflowers included in this guide were photographed from the Central Rocky Mountains of Wyoming to the Southern Rocky Mountains of Colorado. Images were taken over a period of five summers and feature the most common plus a few uncommon wildflowers that one may encounter in the high meadows, along trails, and roadsides. All plants are native to the Rocky Mountains unless stated otherwise.

From the many plant species in the Rocky Mountains, a little over 270 are featured in this book. Plants were chosen by how common they are, how noticeable they are, and some were chosen by their unique properties.

Flowers are organized by color as an aid to locating an unknown variety. Shades and colors may vary, so one should rely on the description, appearance, and location of the flower as well.

Colorado- Southern Rocky Mountain Life Zone

1. Foothills 5,000 - 8,000 feet
Flowers are abundant and diverse. The zone is characterized by pinyon pine, juniper, oak forests, shrubs, and some areas of Douglas fir. Also, ponderosa pine can also be found at higher elevations.

2. Montane 8,000 - 10,000 feet
This zone has perhaps the greatest variety of wildflowers with open forest groves and a wide range of shrubs. Douglas fir, pines, spruce, and pinyon are along with aspen colonies.

3. Subalpine 10,000 - 11,500 feet
With more precipitation, and snow runoff streams and springs, meadows are covered with a vast variety of wildflowers. Many conifers, including spruce, fir and pines, bristlecone and limber pines can be spotted on rocky slopes along with patches of blue and Engelmann spruces.

4. Alpine, above 11,500 feet
This zone extends from the timberline or treeline to the highest altitudes. The tundra is a treeless area with low-growing grasses and shrubs. There is little soil to grow on and dwarf wildflower patches have adapted to the severe environment to bloom only for a short period during the peak of summer.

Please note: Life zones differ somewhat in altitude between the Southern Rocky Mountains (Colorado) and the Central Rocky Mountains (Wyoming).

Table of Contents

Index

Watch where you step!

Rugged plants in the high alpine zone endure year-round sub-zero temperatures, tremendous winds and snow lasting up to eight months. Even though some of these plants have survived for hundreds of years, they can die if stepped on; or, they can be smothered by thrown-away debris that blocks sunlight and precious water needed for growth.

Parts of a Flower

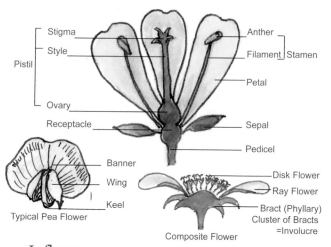

Stigma
Style
Pistil
Ovary
Receptacle
Anther
Filament | Stamen
Petal
Sepal
Pedicel

Banner
Wing
Keel

Typical Pea Flower

Disk Flower
Ray Flower
Bract (Phyllary)
Cluster of Bracts
=Involucre

Composite Flower

Inflorescences = Group or cluster of flowers on a stem

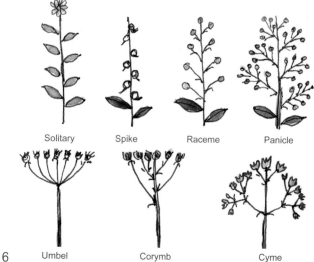

Solitary

Spike

Raceme

Panicle

Umbel

Corymb

Cyme

Leaf Shapes and Arrangements

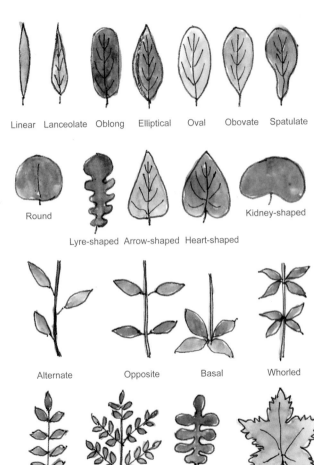

Linear Lanceolate Oblong Elliptical Oval Obovate Spatulate

Round

Lyre-shaped Arrow-shaped Heart-shaped Kidney-shaped

Alternate Opposite Basal Whorled

Pinnate Bi-pinnate Pinnatifid Palmate

Globeflower (American Globeflower)

Trollius laxus (Synonym: *Trollius albiflorus*)
Buttercup Family - Ranunculaceae

Globeflowers appear in clumps as snow melts on mountain slopes. Saucer-shaped flowers, up to 1 1/2 inches across, are on single stalks from 4 to 16 inches tall. Flowers have 5 to 9 white to cream-colored petal-like sepals around a center with multiple yellow stamens. Leaves are alternately arranged on long stalks and are palmately divided into 5 to 7 deeply-toothed parts.
Habitat: Wet areas around streams and in meadows
Life Zone: Montane to subalpine
Flowering Time: Summer

Marsh Marigold
(White Marsh Marigold)
Caltha leptosepala (Syn: *Psychrophila leptosepala*)
Buttercup Family - Ranunculaceae

White saucer-shaped flowers have 5 to 12 petal-like sepals surrounding central disks with many yellow stamens. Leaves are basal, thick, and heart-shaped with visible veins and wavy, sometimes toothed margins. Marsh Marigold grows from 1 to 8 inches tall and has erect leafless flower stalks.
Habitat: Marshes, wet meadows, and along streams
Life Zone: Montane to alpine
Flowering Time: Late spring to late summer

Ocean Spray (Mountain Spray, Rock Spirea)
Holodiscus dumosus
(Synonym: *Holodiscus discolor*)
Rose Family - Rosaceae

Ocean Spray is a shrub that grows to 5 feet tall in rocky outcrops and has dark red twigs and gray branchlets. Native Americans used the branches to make arrow shafts. Many tiny pink to whitish flowers form cone-shaped drooping clusters up to 8 inches long. Leaves are elliptical, up to 2 inches long, with toothed margins.
Habitat: *Rocky slopes and canyon walls*
Life Zone: *Foothills to montane*
Flowering Time: *Summer*

Corn Lily (False Hellebore)
Veratrum californicum
(Synonym: *Veratrum tenuipetalum*)
Lily Family - Liliaceae

(APG III: False Hellebore Family - Melanthiaceae)

This hardy plant can grow up to 7 feet tall and fill vast areas of wetlands with its corn-like leaves and stalks. It has small white to greenish star-shaped flowers with dark green centers that grow in thick clusters on branched panicles. The plant is poisonous, the roots and young shoots most toxic. As the Corn Lily matures, however, it becomes less toxic, usually after a frost.

Habitat: Wet soils around streams and in wetlands
Life Zone: Montane to subalpine
Flowering Time: Summer to early fall

Tall Cottongrass

Slender Cottongrass

Tall Cottongrass
(Cottonsedge, Bogwool)
Eriophorum angustifolium
Sedge Family - Cyperaceae

Tall Cottongrass is a sedge that grows in wetlands and peat bogs. The flowering stems, from 8 to 24 inches high, have 3 to 5 white, fluffy cotton-like blooms nodding from their tops. Leaves are mainly basal and grass-like and have finely rough-toothed margins. Stems have edges. Slender Cottongrass, *Eriophorum gracile,* is rare in Colorado.
Habitat: Cool, wet sites, often in low standing water
Life Zone: Foothills to alpine
Flowering Time: Late spring to summer

Mariposa Lily

(Gunnison's Sego Lily)
Calochortus gunnisonii
Lily Family - Liliaceae

This native perennial flower grows up to 18 inches tall. It has a slim long stem and narrow grass-like leaves up to 8 inches long. The lily's goblet-like head is approximately 2 inches across and has three fan-shaped petals and 3 whitish or pale green sepals. Petals have dark brown spots and yellow hairs in the center.
Habitat: *Sunny meadows, slopes, and open forests*
Life Zone: *Foothills to montane*
Flowering Time: *Summer*

13

Common Alp Lily (Alpine Lily)
Lloydia serotina
Lily Family - Liliaceae

Alp Lilies have dainty drooping flowerheads, 3/4 inch across, with 3 petals and 3 sepals that are white with greenish bases and purplish veins. Leaves are grass-like, up to 6 inches long. Plants grow from 2 to 7 inches high, sometimes in groupings in meadows, but they can also be inconspicuous if tucked in among rocks in their alpine environment.

Habitat: *Rock fields, cliffs, and high sunny meadows*
Life Zone: *Alpine*
Flowering Time: *Early to late summer*

Mountain Death Camas (Wand Lily)
Anticlea elegans (Syn: *Zigadenus elegans*)
Lily Family - Liliaceae

(APG III: False Hellebore Family - Melanthiaceae)

All parts of these elegant plants are very poisonous and bulbs are deadly if ingested. Saucer-like flowers are up to 3/4 inch wide, have 6 points, and grow in a long cluster atop a slender stem from 12 to 20 inches tall. Flowers are cream-white to green-white with a green gland at the base of each petal. Basal leaves are smooth and linear with parallel veins.

Habitat: *Along streams, forest openings, meadows*
Life Zone: *Montane to alpine*
Flowering Time: *Summer to fall*

White Loco

Loco color variations

Loco seed pods

White Loco
(Rocky Mountain Locoweed)
Oxytropis sericea
Pea Family - Fabaceae

Loco plants have numerous white flowers with purple-tipped keels in dense clusters atop leafless stalks. Leaves are pinnately compound with silver-colored leaflets. Loco is toxic to livestock and causes them to go crazy, "loco". White Loco often hybridizes with Lambert's Loco, *Oxytropis lambertii,* producing colors ranging from white, blue, magenta and purple.
Habitat: Gravelly soils, shrublands, open meadows
Life Zone: Foothills to subalpine
Flowering Time: Late spring to late summer

Mountain Valerian
Valeriana acutiloba (Syn: *Valeriana capitata*)
Valerian Family - Valerianaceae

Valerian blooms in lower mountain meadows and its ball-like flowerheads are composed of tiny clusters of tubular white or pinkish flowers with exerted stamens. Upper leaves on stems are few and opposite and larger lower leaves surround the base of the plant, which grows up to 2 feet tall. Valerian plant roots are used for nerve tonics or as mild sedatives.
Habitat: Wet meadows, streambanks, woodlands
Life Zone: Montane to subalpine
Flowering Time: Early to late summer

Cow Parsnip
Heracleum maximum
(Syn: *Heracleum sphondylium*)
Parsley Family - Apiaceae

The Latin name for this plant is appropriate as this Herculean plant can grow up to 6 feet tall. Small white flowers with 5 petals are grouped on umbels up to 12 inches across. Leaves can be platter-sized and are alternate and compound with 3 to 5 lobes similar to a giant maple leaf. Leaves, roots and stems are forage for bears and elk.

Habitat: *Wet meadows, streambanks, willow thickets*
Life Zone: *Foothills to subalpine*
Flowering Time: *Summer*

Alpine Sandwort
(Alpine Stichwort, Twinflower Sandwort)
Minuartia obtusiloba
Pink Family - Caryophyllaceae

This mat-forming plant can dot large areas on alpine tundra, but seldom grows taller than 2 inches. Small 3/8-inch white flowers have 5 petals with irregular edges and 5 yellow-green sepals. Basal leaves with blunt tips form a dense mat just below multiple blossoms. Alpine Sandwort, like Moss Campion and Alpine Phlox, thrives in alpine environments.
Habitat: Dry, sandy or rocky soils
Life Zone: Alpine
Flowering Time: Summer to fall

Arctic Gentian

(Whitish Gentian)

Gentiana algida (Synonym: *Gentianodes algida*)

Gentian Family - Gentianaceae

Arctic Gentians are among the latest summer bloomers. Although generally no more than 6 inches high, they are easily seen because the large, tubular flowers (2 inches long) grow in clumps. White to greenish pleated petals have deep purple streaks outside and are speckled inside and out. Leaves are narrow and oblong up to 3 inches long. "Algida" means cold in Latin.

Habitat: *By streamsides, in meadows, and moist sites*

Life Zone: *Subalpine to alpine*

Flowering Time: *Summer to fall*

Bittercress

(Heartleaf Bittercress)
Cardamine cordifolia
Mustard Family - Brassicaceae

This native perennial grows in large patches on stems up to 30 inches tall. Brilliant white flowers, 3/4 inch long, are cross-shaped with indented petals. Leaves, more or less heart-shaped with jagged or wavy margins, are usually plentiful and are edible. Bittercress plants often appear after snow melt and flower along the banks of mountain streams.

Habitat: Along streamsides and wet forests
Life Zone: Montane to alpine
Flowering Time: Summer to fall

Black-headed Daisy

Erigeron melanocephalus
Sunflower Family - Asteraceae

Single, small flowerheads form on 2 to 6-inch tall stems. Bright white ray flowers with yellow disk flower centers are up to 1 1/2 inches across and have bracts covered with dense black hairs. Basal leaves are on stalks and have rounded tips. Stem leaves are smaller toward the top of the stem.

Habitat: Meadows, gravelly soils, and grassy areas
Life Zone: Subalpine to alpine
Flowering Time: Summer to late summer

Oxeye Daisy (Common Daisy)
Leucanthemum vulgare
Sunflower Family - Asteraceae

Oxeye Daisies grow up to 2 feet tall and have oblong leaves that are serrate or dentate and up to 5 inches long. Flowerheads, approximately 2 1/2 inches across have 25 or more white ray petals and yellow disk centers. Introduced from Europe and Asia, these plants grow in dense clusters that are difficult to contain. Oxeye Daisys are invasive plants and considered noxious weeds in Colorado.

Habitat: *Along roadsides, fields, and pastures*
Life Zone: *Foothills to subalpine*
Flowering Time: *Summer to fall*

ball-like fruit

Virgin's Bower
(Western White Clematis)
Clematis ligusticifolia
Buttercup Family - Ranunculaceae

This showy vine can grow to 20 feet long and cover shrubs and trees. Flowers, 1/2 to 3/4 inches with 5 petal-like sepals and yellow stamens, form loose, round clusters up to 8 inches across. Compound leaves are triangular divided into 5 to 7 notched leaflets from 1 to 3 inches long. Fuzzy, ball-like fruit appears in summer.
Habitat: Streamsides, creeks, and ravines
Life Zone: Plains to foothills
Flowering Time: Spring to early fall

24

Hooded Lady's-Tresses
(Irish Lady's Tresses)
Spiranthes romanzoffiana
Orchid Family - Orchidaceae

Spirals of this white flower are unmistakable. Plants are up to 18 inches tall with 4 to 6 inch flower spikes. Numerous wax-like blossoms circle the central stalk of this orchid. Flower petals are triangular with the bottom petal forming an oblong lip. Long narrow leaves are mostly basal, often inrolled, and stand upright.
Habitat: Wet meadows, bogs, and fens
Life Zone: Montane to subalpine
Flowering Time: Summer to late summer

25

Tailed Seed Pod

Mountain Dryad

(Mountain Avens, Alpine Dryad)
Dryas octopetala
Rose Family - Rosaceae

Mountain Dryad is a mat-forming miniature shrub (4 to 8 inches high) with creamy white flowers, 1 1/2 inches wide. Petals (usually 8 in number) surround yellow stamens. Thick leaves have an embossed leather-like surface, scalloped edges, and blunt tips. When flowers mature, they produce unique tailed seeds.

Habitat: Exposed ridges and slopes
Life Zone: Alpine
Flowering Time: Early to late summer

26

Late blooming color

American Bistort (Knotweed, Snakeweed)
Bistorta bistortoides
(Synonym: *Polygonum bistortoides*)
Buckwheat Family - Polygonaceae

American Bistort is actually a dense cluster of tiny white flowers with 5 white sepals and stamens that stick out on a tall, thin stem. Plant grows from 8 to 24 inches with a 1 to 2-inch flower spike. Leaves are long and narrow, grass-like, and mostly basal. Pants may grow singly, but are most often in large groupings.
Habitat: Meadows, streambanks, and shady woods
Life Zone: Subalpine to alpine
Flowering Time: Early to late summer

Field Bindweed (Field Morning Glory)
Convolvulus arvensis
Morning Glory Family - Convolvulaceae

Funnel-shaped white to pale pink flowers (up to 1 1/2 inches across) grow in large tangled mats along the ground or entwine around shrubs and fences. Leaves are triangular and attached alternately along the twisted stem. Vines forms dense tangles that crowd out native vegetation. Its root system is extensive and resists mechanical and chemical control efforts. It is an invasive noxious weed in Colorado.

Habitat: *Roadsides, fields, and disturbed soils*
Life Zone: *Foothills*
Flowering Time: *Summer to fall*

Yarrow (Western or Common Yarrow, Plumajillo)
Achillea millefolium (Syn: *Achillea lanulosa*)
Sunflower Family - Asteraceae

This very common wildflower, 1 to 3 feet high, has a tight, flat terminal cluster of flowers approximately 2 to 4 inches across. Each tiny flower, 1/4 inch, has 4 to 6 petals. Leaves are soft and fern-like, around 6 inches long, finely divided and feathery. Yarrow is a medicinal plant that has been used for thousands of years to treat everything from insect bites to reducing blood clotting time. Can be also observed with pink blossoms.
Habitat: Meadows, open fields, trails, and roadsides
Life Zone: Foothills to montane
Flowering Time: Late spring to fall

29

Tasselflower (Brickellbush)
Brickellia grandiflora
Sunflower Family - Asteraceae

This perennial grows up to 36 inches tall and has an erect, branched, and leafy stem. Leaves are alternate and triangular up to 5 inches long with deeply-toothed edges. Numerous nodding flowerheads (no ray flowers) up to 2 inches long are white to yellowish. Tea made from this plant has been used to help regulate blood sugar levels with insulin resistant diabetes.
Habitat: *Rocky areas on cliffs, slopes, and in canyons*
Life Zone: *Foothills to montane*
Flowering Time: *Summer*

Inset of leaves
Photo © courtesy of Al Schneider

Rattlesnake-Plantain (Rattlesnake Orchid)
Goodyera oblongifolia
Orchid Family - Orchidaceae

A spike of white, to green or pinkish flowers are arranged in one direction or spiral around a slender stem from 6 to 12 inches tall. Petals and a sepal cover the lower lip of the flower like a hood. Thick evergreen leaves form a basal rosette. Dark green leaves have prominent midribs streaked with white that help in finding and identifying this orchid.

Habitat: Shaded areas under conifers, cool ravines
Life Zone: Foothills to subalpine
Flowering Time: Summer to fall

31

Sickletop Lousewort
(Rams-horn, Parrot's-Beak)
Pedicularis racemosa
Figwort Family - Scrophulariaceae
(APG III: Broomrape Family - Orobanchaceae)

Names for this perennial refer to its unusual curved flower shape. The upper lip curves into a sickle-shape. This native plant has a cluster of white flowers along a central stalk that is 6 to 20 inches tall. Leaves are finely-toothed, lance-shaped, with touches of red or maroon.
Habitat: Along trails, on slopes, and open forests
Life Zone: Montane to subalpine
Flowering Time: Mid to late summer

Porter's Lovage (Osha, Wild Lovage)
Ligusticum porteri
Parsley Family - Apiaceae

Tiny white flowers with a spicy/celery smell grow in flat-topped umbels on stalks that can be 3 to 6 feet tall. Leaves are compound and fern-like. Lovage has been used for medicinal purposes for hundreds of years. Lovage closely resembles Poison Hemlock so one should use caution in identifying the plant. Porter's Lovage grows throughout the Rocky Mountains.
Habitat: Aspen groves, moist meadows, forest openings
Life Zone: Foothills to subalpine
Flowering Time: Summer to fall

33

Alpine Spring Beauty

Lance-leaf Spring Beauty

Alpine Spring Beauty (Fell-fields Claytonia)
Claytonia megarhiza
Purslane Family - Portulacaceae

Lovely, 1/2 to 3/4 inch wide, 5-petalled white to pink flowers with red veins seem somewhat out of place in their harsh, alpine environment. Plants grow from 2 to 5 inches tall. Basal leaves are succulent and form a rosette. As the plant ages, leaves turn from red to green. Lance-leaf Spring Beauty, *Claytonia lanceolata,* has lance-shaped basal and stem leaves, slightly notched petals, and can grow at lower altitudes.

Habitat: *Rocky, gravelly soils and rock crevices*
Life Zone: *Alpine*
34 **Flowering Time:** *Summer to fall*

Fendler's Sandwort
Eremogone fendleri
(Synonym: *Arenaria fendleri*)
Pink Family - Caryophyllaceae

These common native plants were named for Augustus Fendler, a botanical collector who gathered specimens in the 1840s. Tiny white flowers, 1/4 to 1/2 inch wide, have pink to maroon-tipped anthers that look like spots at first glance. Plants grow from 4 to 12 inches tall and have narrow, grass-like leaves.
Habitat: *Forest openings, high mountain meadows*
Life Zone: *Montane to alpine*
Flowering Time: *Summer*

Tufted Evening Primrose

(Stemless Evening-Primrose)
Oenothera caespitosa
Evening Primrose Family - Onagraceae

Large, bright white blossoms, up to 4 inches across, grow close to the ground above a rosette of jagged basal leaves with pointed tips. Heart-shaped petals change from white to pink with age. Flowers bloom late in the day and wilt by noon of the next day.
Habitat: *Disturbed areas, hillsides, sand, loose gravel*
Life Zone: *Foothills to montane*
Flowering Time: *Late spring to summer*

Richardson's Geranium
(White Geranium, White Crane's-Bill)
Geranium richardsonii
Geranium Family - Geraniaceae

White flowers, up to 1 inch wide, have 5 petals with pink to purple veins. Plants have erect stems and can grow to 3 feet tall. Leaves have 5 to 7 pointed lobes. Besides the white blossoms, plants are easily noticed by their leaves that turn bright red in the fall.
Habitat: Shady areas, along streams, woodlands
Life Zone: Foothills to subalpine
Flowering Time: Summer

Bladder Campion
Silene latifolia
(Syn: *Lychnis alba*)
Pink Family - Caryophyllaceae

Introduced originally from Europe, Asia, and Africa, this non-native plant grows to 35 inches tall and has flowers with 5 white lobed, deeply notched petals. The calyx is hairy, veined and inflated. Stem leaves are opposite, up to 4 inches long, and oblong.
Habitat: *Fields, roadsides, and disturbed areas*
Life Zone: *Foothills*
Flowering Time: *Summer*

Mouse-Ear Chickweed
(Field Chickweed)
Cerastium arvense
(Synonym: *Cerastium strictum*)
Pink Family - Caryophyllaceae

Small white to pinkish flowers have 5 notched and rounded petals that resemble mouse ears. Blossoms with greenish-yellow stamens are 1/2 inch wide on straight stems varying in size up to 10 inches tall. Linear leaves are narrow and opposite. Chickweed sometimes grows in large, sprawling patches.
Habitat: Meadows and forest openings
Life Zone: Foothills to alpine
Flowering Time: Spring to summer

39

White Peavine
(White-flowered Lathyrus, Nevada Pea)
Lathyrus lanszwertii (Syn: *Lathyrus leucanthus*)
Pea Family - Fabaceae

White flowers with pink or purple veins are up to 1 inch long and grow in small groups on vine-like stems. Leaves are compound with sometimes up to 10 leaflets growing to 3 inches long with tendrils replacing the tip leaflet. The size and color of petals and the shape and number of leaflets varies. Peavine often covers large areas.
Habitat: *Aspen groves, ravines, and meadows*
Life Zone: *Montane to subalpine*
Flowering Time: *Late spring to summer*

Alpine Phlox (Dwarf Phlox)
Phlox condensata
Phlox Family - Polemoniaceae

Alpine Phlox is a common perennial dwarf-like plant that forms cushions to over a foot in diameter with short, up to 1 inch stems extending above a thick mat of leaves. Sweet-smelling white (can have a pink or blue tinge) flat flowers, approximately 1/4 inch across, have 5 petals and hairy, sticky calyxes. Leaves are narrow, fleshy, overlapping, and sharp-pointed.
Habitat: *Gravelly slopes and rocky soils*
Life Zone: *Alpine*
Flowering Time: *Summer*

41

Whiplash Daisy
(Trailing Fleabane)
Erigeron flagellaris
Sunflower Family - Asteraceae

Small white flowers (sometimes pink or light blue) up to 3/4 inch in diameter grow on single stems with sparse hairs that are up to 8 inches tall. Flowerheads have more than 50 ray flowers surrounding greenish-yellow center disks. Leaves are numerous and narrow with rough edges. Plants send out leafy runners that root and may form large colonies.

Habitat: Hillsides, meadows, and exposed sites
Life Zone: Foothills to subalpine
Flowering Time: Spring to summer

Case's Corydalis (Case's Fitweed)
Corydalis caseana subspecies *brandegeei*
Fumitory Family - Fumariaceae

This massive plant can grow up to 6 feet tall. Flowers
in elongated clusters are approximately 3/4 inch long
with spurs and vary in color from white to pink to purple.
Leaves are large, up to 12 inches long, and pinnately
divided with leaflets about 1 inch long. Thick stems up
to 1/2 inch in diameter support the large leafy plants.
Case's Corydalis is rare in parts of Colorado.
Habitat: Aspen, spruce-fir woodlands, wet meadows
Life Zone: Montane to subalpine
Flowering Time: Summer

Bunchberry (Dwarf Dogwood)
Cornus canadensis
Dogwood Family - Cornaceae

This low-growing native perennial has a flower similar to a miniature dogwood. A large central flower cluster is surrounded by 4 white petal-like bracts. The plant has a circular arrangement of 4 to 6 oval-shaped shiny leaves with a few deep veins. Bunchberry grows to a height of approximately 8 inches. Bright red berries form on the plant by midsummer.
Habitat: *Partial shade in forests*
Life Zone: *Subalpine*
Flowering Time: *Early summer*

Northern Bedstraw

Galium boreale
(Synonym: *Gallium septentrionale*)
Madder Family - Rubiaceae

Sweet-smelling tiny white flowers grow in pyramid-shaped clusters atop erect stems, 8 to 20 inches tall. Flowers have four petals, 4 stamens and 2 styles. Stems are hollow and square and have 4 slender lance-shaped leaves attached in whorls at the nodes. Bedstraw was used by pioneers as a soft bedding stuffing.

Habitat: *Moist meadows and woodlands*
Life Zone: *Montane to subalpine*
Flowering Time: *Summer to late summer*

Spotted Saxifrage

(Dotted Saxifrage)
Saxifraga austromontana
(Syn: *Saxifraga bronchialis*)
Saxifrage Family - Saxifragaceae

Tiny evergreen perennials grow from 3 to 6 inches high and have branched flower clusters with flower stems rising from a cushion of moss-like basal leaves. White flowers, approximately 3/8 inch across, have 5 petals dotted with orange to pink to purple spots. Linear-shaped leaves are alternate and have short spines at the tips.
Habitat: *Dry areas, along trails, and rocky slopes*
Life Zone: *Montane to alpine*
Flowering Time: *Summer*

Pearly Everlasting
Anaphalis margaritacea
Sunflower Family - Asteraceae

Composite disk flowers form round clusters of flowers atop woolly stems. Small individual flowerheads are composed of pearl-white bracts surrounding yellow to brownish disk flowers. Distinctive pale blue-green leaves are hairy or woolly underneath and arranged alternately along the stem. "Margaritacea" means "pearl" in Latin.
Habitat: *Along trails, roads, and in meadows*
Life Zone: *Montane*
Flowering Time: *Summer to fall*

Engelmann's Aster
Eucephalus engelmannii
Sunflower Family - Asteraceae

Tall, airy perennial is notable with its large, loose flower heads. White ray flowers, that turn pink with age, often appear twisted. Central yellow disk appears small compared to the disheveled rays. Leaves are lance-shaped, alternate, net-veined and hairy beneath. This plant was named after the 19th century botanist, George Engelmann, who discovered hundreds of new species.
Habitat: In aspen groves, ravines, forest openings
Life Zone: Foothills to subalpine
Flowering Time: Late spring to mid-summer

Wild Candytuft (Mountain Candytuft)
Noccaea fendleri (Synonym: *Noccaea montana*)
Mustard Family - Brassicaceae

Intense white flowers in tight clusters grow on stems that reach 10 inches tall. Cross-shaped 4-petalled blossoms are 1/4 inch long with 4 pointed sepals. Leaves along the stem are clasping and alternate. Basal leaves are spoon-shaped. Candytuft often grows with few other plants around it and can begin blooming when only an inch tall. It often grows in large patches.
Habitat: Hillsides, open woods, and shrublands
Life Zone: Foothills to alpine
Flowering Time: Spring to fall

Choke Cherry
Prunus virginiana   (Syn: *Padus virginiana*)
Rose Family - Rosaceae

Chokecherry shrubs or trees grow from 3 to 24 feet tall and produce bountiful red to black small cherries for birds and wildlife in summer. Massive blooms, 3" to 6" long, are composed of numerous white to cream-colored saucer-shaped flowers forming elongated clusters. Oval-shaped leaves, 2 to 5 inches long, are alternate with pointed tips and finely-toothed edges.
Habitat: Streamsides and open woods
Life Zone: Foothills to montane
Flowering Time: Spring to early summer

Miner's Candle
Oreocarya virgata   (Syn: *Cryptantha virgata*)
Borage Family - Boraginaceae

These distinctive plants have long, single unbranched stems up to 24 inches tall. Stiff hairs and bristles that cover stems and leaves give the plant a soft, grayish look, but the plant is certainly not soft to touch. Small white flowers with 5 petals are in clusters surrounded by long leaf-like bracts that extend beyond them.
Habitat: Woodlands and gravelly slopes
Life Zone: Foothills to montane
Flowering Time: Spring to late summer

Bog Orchid
Platanthera aquilonis
(Syn: *Limnorchis hyperborea*)
Orchid Family - Orchidaceae

These greenish-white flowers with spurs on the back of the blossoms grow along stout stalks to over a foot tall. Lance-shaped leaves are larger at the base and become smaller as they grow up the stem. Even though this orchid can grow in patches, it is often overlooked because it blends so well with its surroundings.

Habitat: *Wet meadows, marshes, fens, streambanks*
Life Zone: *Foothills to subalpine*
Flowering Time: *Summer*

Elk Thistle (Colorado Thistle)
Cirsium scariosum
(Synonym: *Cirsium coloradense*)
Sunflower Family - Asteraceae

This thistle with many names is a leafy plant that can grow up to 48 inches tall or hug the ground in a rosette of leaves. Individual disk flowers are white to purplish color and up to 2 inches across. Spine-tipped leaves are simple, alternate, lobed and clasp the stem. Both stems and leaves are covered with long white hairs extending into the flowerheads.

Habitat: Aspen groves, meadows, streambanks
Life Zone: Foothills to subalpine
Flowering Time: Summer to late summer

Cutleaf Evening Primrose
Oenothera coronopifolia
Evening Primrose Family - Onagraceae

White flowers up to 1 1/2 inches across have 4 petals and stamens that extend beyond the flower. Blossoms change to pink as they age. Plants grow up to 12 inches high. Cutleaf Evening Primrose is distinguished from other members of its family by its stringy finely cut leaves on yellowish stems. Plants spread from taproot and form colonies.
Habitat: Gravelly roadsides and sandy open areas
Life Zone: Foothills to montane
Flowering Time: Late spring to summer

White Prickly Poppy
(Prickly Poppy)
Argemone polyanthemos
(Synonym: *Argemone platyceras*)
Poppy Family - Papaveraceae

White, showy blooms up to 4 inches across consist of
4 to 6 wrinkled, paper-like petals that surround a yellow
ball-shaped center of stamens. Leaves are lobed, up to
8 inches long, and have extremely sharp yellow spines
along the veins and edges. Oval seed pods are also
prickly. Plant grows over 3 feet tall and is poisonous.
Habitat: *Sandy, dry areas along roadsides, hillsides*
Life Zone: *Foothills*
Flowering Time: *Spring to fall*

55

Yucca (Soapweed Yucca, Spanish Bayonet)
Yucca glauca
Agave Family - Agavaceae

Yucca is an evergreen plant, 1 to 5 feet tall composed of a dense growth of narrow, needle-pointed leaves with a single flower stalk. Greenish-white flowers 2 to 3 inches long on a stout stem extend above the leaves. Blossoms are composed of tepals surrounding 6 stamens and a green style in a cluster. Native Americans used leaves for cordage and made soap from roots. Flowers and seed pods have been cooked and eaten.

Habitat: *Dry open sites and rocky areas*
Life Zone: *Foothills*
Flowering Time: *Late spring to summer*

56

Alpine Pussytoes

Rosy Pussytoes

Tall Pussytoes

Tall Pussytoes
Antennaria pulcherrima
Sunflower Family - Asteraceae

Pussytoes are easy to spot with their tight clusters of ray flowers that resemble pads on a cat's paw. Most plants have basal and stem leaves that are woolly. Tall Pussytoes grow to 16 inches high. Upper Inset: Alpine Pussytoes, *Antennaria media*, grows up to 3 inches tall. Lower Inset: Rosy Pussytoes, *Antennaria rosea,* has disk flowers that are surrounded by pink bracts.
Habitat: Dry meadows and open forests
Life Zone: Montane to subalpine
Flowering Time: Summer

White Checkermallow
(White Checkerbloom)
Sidalcea candida
Mallow Family - Malvaceae

White Checkermallow grows to heights of approximately 3 feet and has mostly smooth leaves that vary greatly. Basal leaves are toothed and shallowly lobed and upper leaves are palmate. Flowers, up to 2 inches wide, have 5 separate petals, usually white or sometimes pinkish or cream-colored with age, and a column of stamens.
Habitat: Wet meadows, near streams, and lakes
Life Zone: Montane
Flowering Time: Summer

Red Elderberry

Sambucus racemosa (Syn: *S. microbotrys*)
Honeysuckle Family - Caprifoliaceae

(APG III: Muskroot Family - Adoxaceae)

Red Elderberry shrubs have red stems with many branches and grow to heights of 3 to 10 feet. When blooming, the bush is covered with tiny white flowers in large showy clusters up to 5 inches across. Leaves are opposite and compound with 5 or more leaflets all with toothed margins. Fruit is red to purplish-black berries in dense clusters.

Habitat: *Along trails, meadows, and open woods*
Life Zone: *Montane to subalpine*
Flowering Time: *Summer*

59

Wood Nymph (Single Delight)

Moneses uniflora (Synonym: *Pyrola uniflora*)
Wintergreen Family - Pyrolaceae

(APG III: Heath Family - Ericaceae)

This tiny star-like flower, up to 3/4 inch across, is often overlooked because of its small size. A single white deeply nodding flower grows on a stem up to 5 inches tall above evergreen basal leaves. Petals are white, waxy, and fused at the base. Blossoms are fragrant with a scent similar to Lily-of-the-Valley.

Habitat: *Moist forests, shaded areas, along streams*
Life Zone: *Montane to subalpine*
Flowering Time: *Summer*

Boulder Raspberry

Wild Red Raspberry

Boulder Raspberry

(Rocky Mountain Raspberry)
Rubus deliciosus (Syn: *Oreobatus deliciosus*)
Rose Family - Rosaceae

This perennial shrub grows up to 5 feet tall. Its white flowers, 1 to 3 inches across, have slightly wrinkled petals. Leaves are deeply lobed with toothed edges. Branches have no bristles and the fruit has little taste. Inset: Wild Red Raspberry, *Rubus idaeus,* is edible, has bristles, and egg-shaped pointed leaves with toothed edges.
Habitat: Dry hillsides, along roads, and on slopes
Life Zone: Foothills to montane
Flowering Time: Late spring to summer

61

Starry Lily-of-the-Valley (Star Lily)
Maianthemum stellatum
(Syn: *Smilacina stellata*)
Lily Family - Liliaceae

(APG III: Butcher's Broom Family - Ruscaceae)

This dainty perennial often grows in colonies of dozens of plants. Single, unbranched, arching stems, have a small, terminal cluster of white, star-shaped flowers consisting of 6 tepals (petals and sepals look the same). Oval to lance-shaped leaves with parallel veins are alternately arranged along an 8 to 10 inch long stem.
Habitat: *Moist soils in woods and along streams*
Life Zone: *Montane to subalpine*
Flowering Time: *Spring to summer*

Small flowered Grass-of-Parnassus

Fringed Grass-of-Parnassus
Parnassia fimbriata
Saxifrage Family - Saxifragaceae

(APG III: Grass of Parnassus Family - Parnassiaceae)

Small star-like white flowers grow on single stems above kidney or heart-shaped, glossy leaves. Petals have greenish yellow veins and are fringed at the base. Inset: Small-flowered Grass-of-Parnassus, *Parnassia parviflora*, is similar, but does not have fringed petals and its leaves are more elongated and oval.

Habitat: *Mossy banks of streams and wet meadows*
Life Zone: *Montane to subalpine*
Flowering Time: *Summer to early fall*

63

Redroot Buckwheat
Eriogonum racemosum
Buckwheat Family - Polygonaceae

Redroot buckwheat can cover fields with elongated flower clusters that are white and tinged with pink. Flowers grow on stiff, leafless stems above basal, woolly, elliptical leaves. Individual flowers have 6 petals with darker middle stripes and pink-tipped stamens. Vertical-standing leaves are often found without flower stems. This native plant grows from 6 to 40 inches tall.
Habitat: Dry meadows, sandy soils, and roadsides
Life Zone: Foothills to montane
Flowering Time: Summer to early fall

Wild Cosmos

Hymenopappus newberryi
Sunflower Family - Asteraceae

Wild Cosmos grows from 8 to 24 inches high usually on south-facing hillsides. It has mostly deeply divided basal leaves plus a few similar leaves along the stem. White ray petals are wide, creased, lightly notched, and surround a yellow central disk. Varieties of cosmos seeds, available in nurseries, produce deer-resistant garden plants. Wild Cosmos is found in only a few counties in Colorado and New Mexico.

Habitat: *Hillsides and open woods*
Life Zone: *Montane*
Flowering Time: *Summer*

Cutleaf Daisy (Dwarf Mountain Fleabane)
Erigeron compositus
Sunflower Family - Asteraceae

Cutleaf Daisy grows up to 8 inches tall on erect, nearly leafless stems. Small flowerheads are 3/4 inches across and mostly white, but can be pink, blue, or lavender. Bracts below the flowerheads are quite hairy and red-tipped. Leaves are mostly basal, hairy and fern-like. Plants grow in mats or cushions with flower stems extending above the clusters of sage-colored deeply divided leaves.

Habitat: Dry areas, gravelly soils, and along trails
Life Zone: Foothills to subalpine
Flowering Time: Summer to fall

Round-Leaf Thimbleweed
(Canadian Anemone)
Anemone canadensis
(Syn: *Anemonidium canadense*)
Buttercup Family - Ranunculaceae

Plant has deeply lobed, basal leaves and an 8 inch to 2 foot stem with a whorl of leaves divided in 3 to 5 parts. Single white flower with a center of many stamen appears above the leaf whorl. Palmate leaves have toothed margins and hairs on the underside. Native Americans used parts of the plants for treatment of wounds.
Habitat: Moist meadows, thickets, and around streams
Life Zone: Foothills to montane
Flowering Time: Late spring to summer

Canadian White Violet

Viola canadensis (Syn: *Viola scopulorum*)
Violet Family - Violaceae

Bright white flowers are often seen in large groupings. Plants can grow from 6 and sometimes up to 12 inches tall if conditions are right. Flowers, 3/4 inch across, consist of 5 petals with back sides that are often pink or purple-tinged. Lower 3 petals have fine purple lines leading to the center of the flower. Both basal and stem leaves are alternate and heart-shaped with pointed tips.

Habitat: *Moist soils in woods, often in shade*
Life Zone: *Foothills to montane*
Flowering Time: *Spring to summer*

Longbeak Water-Crowfoot

(Water Buttercup)
Ranunculus longirostris (Syn: *Batrachium aquatile*)
Buttercup Family - Ranunculaceae

These plants form floating masses in slow-moving streams or ponds. Leaves are mostly submerged, finely divided, and thread-like. Small white flowers, with 5 petals and protruding stamens and pistils, float on the surface of the water. Plants provide important habitats for small fishes and aquatic insects.
Habitat: Slow streams or ditches
Life Zone: Foothills to montane
Flowering Time: Late spring to summer

69

Fendler's Waterleaf
Hydrophyllum fendleri
Waterleaf Family - Hydrophyllaceae
(APG III: Borage Family - Boraginaceae)

These unusual plants grow from 1 to 3 feet tall and have ball-shaped cream to purplish flowerheads with protruding stamens, that appear like pincushions. Leaves are wide and deeply cut into 9 to 13 parts that are roughly serrated. Plants are often unnoticed as they grow with other greenery in moist aspen forests. Flowers appear just above the plant's many leaves.
Habitat: Moist soils in shady woods
Life Zone: *Montane to subalpine*
Flowering Time: *Summer*

Sweet-Flower Rock Jasmine

(Alpine Rock Jasmine)
Androsace chamaejasme
Primrose Family - Primulaceae

Small white flowers, 2 to 8 in a cluster, grow on leafless stems. Individual flowers have 5 wide lobes surrounding a bright yellow center that can turn pink with age. Leaves are basal, narrow, lance-shaped and hairy. Plants sometimes form showy colonies, but are often overlooked because of their small size. Flowers from 1 to 4 inches tall have a scent like tropical jasmine.
Habitat: Rocky slopes and tundra
Life Zone: Subalpine to alpine
Flowering Time: Summer to early fall

71

Cowbane
(Fendler's Cowbane)
Oxypolis fendleri
Parsley Family - Apiaceae

Tiny, delicate white flowers are in loose, open umbels up to 2 inches across. Tall, upright stems to 2 feet tall, have few leaves and are hollow and weak. Leaves on the lower part of the plant are pinnate, oval-shaped and have a single terminal leaflet. Margins may vary from smooth to slightly serrated.

Habitat: *Very wet soils and by streams*
Life Zone: *Montane to subalpine*
Flowering Time: *Early summer to summer*

Snowball Saxifrage (Diamond Saxifrage)
Micranthes rhomboidea
(Syn: *Saxifraga rhomboidea*)
Saxifrage Family - Saxifragaceae

Snowball Saxifrage has diamond-shaped shiny leaves
forming a rosette at the base of the plant. Leafless, erect,
sticky stems from 4 to 12 inches tall are toped with a
snowball of dense small flowers. Flowers have 5 white
petals, and 5 green sepals that grow in a ball-like cluster.
Plants grow singly or in small groupings.
Habitat: Alpine meadows, rocky and gravelly soils
Life Zone: Foothills to alpine
Flowering Time: Summer to fall

Red-osier Dogwood (Western Dogwood)
Cornus alba   (Syn: *Swida sericea*)
Dogwood Family - Cornaceae

This erect to sprawling shrub grows from 3 to 8 feet tall and has distinctive red to purplish branches. Leaves are 1 to 4 inches long with pointed tips and 5 to 7 prominent veins. Small white flowers with 4 oval petals, and 4 stamens form flat-topped clusters. Fruits are fleshy white, sometimes bluish berries. Native people ate the berries and used bark for medicinal purposes. Shrubs are used today for streambank protection
Habitat: Moist soils along streams
Life Zone: Foothills to montane
Flowering Time: Spring to fall

Alpine Bistort

Bistorta vivipara   (Syn: *Polygonum viviparum*)
Buckwheat Family - Polygonaceae

Alpine Bistort grows from 3 to 15 inches tall. Its basal leaves are up to 10 inches log and can be lanceolate, oblong or oval. Terminal flower spikes are composed of tiny white flowers with 5 sepals and protruding stamens. The lower part of the flower cluster and sometimes the entire flower cluster is replaced with bulblets. These bulblets fall to the ground to produce new plants and can be eaten as a nut-like snack.

Habitat: Grassy meadows and rocky areas
Life Zone: Montane to alpine
Flowering Time: Summer to fall

Long Leaf Starwort (Long-stalked Chickweed)
Stellaria longipes
(Syn: *Smilacina stellata*)
Pink Family - Caryophyliaceae

Delicate white terminal flowers have 5 cleft petals. Plants grow from usually 6 inches to sometimes 12 inches tall and have erect stems with narrow lance-shaped opposite leaves. Flowers appear singly or a few together in open clusters, usually with one upright flower per stem. The genus name, *Stellaria*, is Latin for "star".

Habitat: *Open woods and meadows*
Life Zone: *Foothills to alpine*
Flowering Time: *Summer to fall*

Marsh Felwort
Lomatogonium rotatum
Gentian Family - Gentianaceae

This attractive star-shaped flower only grows in a few counties in Colorado and was photographed in Park County. White to pale blue star-shaped blossoms consist of 5 lance-shaped petals, around an extended center. Narrow leaves are smooth and alternate along the stem and form a rosette at the base. Star Gentian is similar in appearance but has blue-grey to purple petals and leaves that are spoon-shaped and mostly basal.

Habitat: *Moist meadows and streamsides*
Life Zone: *Montane to subalpine*
Flowering Time: *Late summer to early fall*

77

Western Peppergrass

(Mountain Pepperplant)
Lepidium montanum
Mustard Family - Brassicaceae

Clusters of tiny white fragrant flowers are atop stems from 10inches to over 4 feet tall. Plants grow usually in group-ings, but sometimes singly. Basal leaves are lobed, the stem leaves are for the most part linear. Seed pods are oval to elliptical and have a peppery smell and taste. Western Peppergrass is highly variable with more than 20 varieties identified.

Habitat: Pinyon/Juniper forests, openings
Life Zone: Foothills to montane
Flowering Time: Summer to fall

Brook Saxifrage
Micranthes odontoloma
Saxifrage Family - Saxifragaceae

Tiny white blossoms appear in a loose panicle on top of tall, branched, leafless reddish stems. Flowers consist of 5 petals, 5 red to purplish sepals, and 10 red-tipped stamens that give the flowers an ornate appearance when viewed with a hand lens. Brook Saxifrage grows to 20 inches tall and has many rounded basal leaves with scalloped edges.
Habitat: Wet meadows, near waterfalls, and streams
Life Zone: Montane to subalpine
Flowering Time: Summer to early fall

Butter Candle

(Cryptantha, Butte Candle)
Cryptantha celeosioides
Borage Family - Boraginaceae

Dainty white flowers with hairy sepals grow in clusters on a 5 to 20 inch tall, unbranched stem. Blossoms consist of 5 rounded petals around a yellow center opening or throat and are clustered around the top of the stem. Basal leaves are spoon-shaped and stem leaves are smaller. Fine hairs on leaves and stem give the plant a fuzzy appearance.

Habitat: Dry soils and open areas
Life Zone: Foothills to montane
Flowering Time: Early summer

Black Henbane

(Stinking Nightshade, Hog Bean)
Hyoscyamus niger
Nightshade Family - Solanaceae

Introduced from Europe, this plant is listed as a noxious weed in Colorado, and other western states. It is highly poisonous. Plant reaches heights of 1 to 3 feet. Leaves have shallow lobes, are coarsely toothed, have sticky hairs, and emit a foul smell. Flowers with 5 petals are cream to yellowish-brown with purple centers and veins. Seed pods are clustered on 2 long rows.

Habitat: *Pastures, roadsides, wetlands, waste areas*
Life Zone: *Foothills to montane*
Flowering Time: *Summer to fall*

Sweet Sand-Verbena

(Snowball Sand-verbena)
Abronia fragrans
Four O'Clock Family - Nyctaginaceae

This sprawling plant grows from 8 to 40 inches tall and has hairy, sticky leaves and stems. Fragrant flowers open late in the day (hence the name Four O'Clock Family) Blossoms are arranged in rounded clusters of individual elongated trumpet-shaped blossoms with 5 small lobes. Leaves are opposite, simple, and egg-shaped to linear.
Habitat: Sandy soils, pinyon-juniper areas
Life Zone: Plains to montane
Flowering Time: Early summer to fall

Drummond's Milkvetch
Astragalus drummondii
Pea Family - Fabaceae

Drummond's Milkvetch has bushy, woolly foliage that appears gray-green in color. Flowers are white to cream to yellowish and hang in dense elongated clusters. Leaves are pinnately divided with 13 to 30 oblong leaflets. Plant grows from 16 to 36 inches high and has thick, hairy stems. Flowers change to hairless pods with a lengthwise groove on one side.
Habitat: *Dry fields and slopes*
Life Zone: *Foothills to montane*
Flowering Time: *Summer*

Annual Sunflower (Common Sunflower)
Helianthus annuus
Sunflower Family - Asteraceae

Commonly covering large areas along roadsides, these erect plants grow from 3 to 6 feet tall. Large flowerhead, usually 1 per stem, has bright yellow rays surrounding a reddish-brown central disk. Bracts and stems are quite hairy. Large egg to heart-shaped leaves with irregularly toothed edges are alternate on upper stem and opposite toward bottom of stem. Seeds are edible like its relative, the garden sunflower.
Habitat: Roadsides and disturbed ares
Life Zone: Foothills
Flowering Time: Summer to fall

Prairie Sunflower

Helianthus petiolaris
Sunflower Family - Asteraceae

Showy yellow flowers grow singly or a few per stem in clumps that look like a small bushes. Prairie Sunflowers can also occur as single plants scattered around. They are similar to Common Sunflowers but are usually shorter, up to 3 feet tall, have more elongated leaves, and smaller flowerheads. Leaves are variable, but usually have wavy edges and a rough texture. Leaf edges and stems are hairy.

Habitat: Roadsides, pinyon-juniper areas
Life Zone: Foothills
Flowering Time: Early summer to fall

Common Tansy (Garden Tansy)
Tanacetum vulgare
Sunflower Family - Asteraceae

Showy, yellow button-like flowerheads consist of small tightly packed disk flowers arranged in flat-topped branching clusters atop stems. Plants grow from 1 1/2 to 6 feet tall and have aromatic fern-like leaves deeply divided into narrow toothed segments. Stems are often purple-red. Common Tansy, introduced from Europe, is considered a noxious weed in Colorado and is poisonous.

Habitat: *Streamsides, pastures, and along roadsides*
Life Zone: *Foothills to montane*
Flowering Time: *Summer to fall*

Nuttall's Violet (Yellow Prairie Violet)
Viola nuttallii
Violet Family - Violaceae

Plants grow from 4 to 8 inches tall with bright yellow flowers nodding atop leafless stems. Flowers consist of 2 backward-curving upper petals and 3 lower petals with purple-striped nectar guides. Basal leaves on stalks are lance-shaped, with conspicuous veins. Leaves are edible and are high in vitamins A and C. However, seeds and roots can cause stomach problems if eaten.

Habitat: Dry soils, forest edges, sagebrush areas
Life Zone: Foothills to montane
Flowering Time: Late spring to summer

87

Clustered Broomrape
Orobanche fasciculata
Broomrape Family - Orobanchaceae

Unique plant grows from 2 to 7 inches tall and is often hidden among other plants. It is a parasite and attaches to various species of sagebrush for nourishment. Stems and bract-like leaves have no green color as they lack chlorophyll. Tube-shaped yellow to brownish-red flowers, 2 to 6 per stem, have 5 lobed petals with glandular hairs.
Habitat: *Dry open sites, sagebrush areas*
Life Zone: *Foothills to montane*
Flowering Time: *Spring to summer*

Greater Bladderwort

(Common Bladderwort)
Utricularia macrorhiza
Bladderwort Family - Lentibulariaceae

Bright, 1/2 inch yellow flowers appear in clusters of 2 to 12 blossoms above the surface of water. Blossoms have a distinctive horn-shaped spur. Leaves, alternate and finely divided, form a web underneath the water. This carnivorous plant has small bladders intermingled with leaves that have tiny openings to trap insects.
Habitat: Shallow water in fens, ponds, and streams
Life Zone: Foothills to montane
Flowering Time: Summer

Yellow Avens
Geum aleppicum
Rose Family - Rosaceae

Bright yellow flowers appear in small clusters and have 5 rounded petals and 5 pointed sepals that are bent backward. Compound basal leaves with coarsely serrated edges are divided in three parts. Tall slender plants are up to 3 feet high and are often found in with moist meadows mixed with grasses. Fruits are globe-shaped seed heads with styles ending in hooks.

Habitat: *Moist areas in meadows or woods*
Life Zone: *Foothills to montane*
Flowering Time: *Spring to late summer*

Creeping Oregon Grape

Mahonia repens   (Syn: *Berberis repens*)
Barberry Family - Berberidaceae

This low-growing evergreen shrub is from 4 to 10 inches tall and has alternate, glossy holly-like leaves. It spreads in groupings close to the ground. Clusters of tiny yellow flowers bloom in spring and are replaced In fall by grape-like clusters of dark blue berries. Leaves change also in fall from green to shades of red. Berries mixed with water and sugar make a refreshing drink.
Habitat: *Wet meadows, near waterfalls, and streams*
Life Zone: *Montane to subalpine*
Flowering Time: *Spring to summer*

Many-flowered Stoneseed
Lithospermum multiflorum
Borage Family - Boraginaceae

Yellow tubular flowers, up to 1/2 inch long, droop or stand out from stems that are upright or leaning in all directions. Stems are hairy and grow up to 2 feet tall in clusters giving the plant a shrub-like appearance. Light green leaves are lance-shaped, hairy, and become smaller toward the top of the stem. Stoneseeds are also known as "Puccoons".

Habitat: *Woods, shrublands, and meadows*
Life Zone: *Foothills to montane*
Flowering Time: *Spring to summer*

Yellow Sweet Clover
Melilotus officinalis
Pea Family - Fabaceae

Tall, sprawling thin-stemmed plant grows up to 6 feet tall. Yellow or white small flowers form spike terminal clusters up to 8 inches long. Leaves are compound, divided into 3 narrow toothed, lance-shaped leaflets Oval-shaped seed pods have a corrugated surface. This non-native plant was once grown as a hay crop, but now has escaped and grows throughout Colorado. Crushed leaves and flowers emit a fresh-mown pasture scent.
Habitat: *Roadsides, open fields, and disturbed soils*
Life Zone: *Plains to montane*
Flowering Time: *Spring to fall*

93

Hairy Evening Primrose
Oenothera villosa
Evening Primrose Family - Onagraceae

Hairy Evening Primrose is a biennial that produces a rosette of leaves the first year and a tall (up to 4 feet), flowering plant the second year. Bright yellow flowers with 4 petals are up to 2 inches wide on top of hairy stems. Blossoms open toward evening and wilt by noon of the following day. Leaves are hairy, lance-shaped, 4 to 8 inches long, and sometimes finely toothed.

Habitat: Roadsides, along fences, and dry slopes
Life Zone: Foothills
Flowering Time: Summer to fall

Woolly Actinea (Stemless Hymenoxys)
Tetraneuris brevifolia (Syn: *Hymenoxys acaulis*)
Sunflower Family - Asteraceae

Yellow flowerheads of this plant are from 1 to 1 1/2
inches across and have notched petals. Silvery-green
basal leaves and stems are covered with fine hairs;
hence the name Woolly Actinea. Although short in
height, approximately 5 inches tall, it often grows in
clumps of eye-catching bright yellow flowers.
Habitat: Sunny dry hillsides, slopes, and rocky areas
Life Zone: Subalpine to alpine
Flowering Time: Summer

Blacktip Senecio (Tall Blacktip Ragwort)
Senecio atratus
Sunflower Family - Asteraceae

Flowerheads are tight clusters of small (1/2 inch wide) ray flowers atop stout stems. Bracts at base of the flowerheads have conspicuous black tips. Leaves are large, up to 12 inches long, and silver-gray colored with toothed margins. Plants form in large clumps and grow from 12 to 30 inches high.
Habitat: Roadsides, trails, and rocky areas
Life Zone: Montane to subalpine
Flowering Time: Summer to early fall

Sulphur-Flower Buckwheat
(Sulphur-Flower)
Eriogonum umbellatum
Buckwheat Family - Polygonaceae

These native perennials have ball-like flower clusters or umbels on 6 to 12 inch tall slender stems. Flower heads consist of many tiny cup-like flowers ranging from bright yellow to cream to pink-tinged and often turn dark red with age. Basal mat-forming lance-shaped leaves are grey-green and woolly.
Habitat: Dry soils, grassy hill sides and shrublands
Life Zone: Foothills to alpine
Flowering Time: Early to late summer

97

Arrowleaf Balsamroot

Balsamorhiza sagittata
Sunflower Family - Asteraceae

Showy flowerheads, 3 to 4 inches across, grow on single stems to 3 feet tall. Both tubular disk florets and the ray florets are yellow. Large, silvery-green leaves are arrow-shaped to triangular and mainly basal. Plants often grow in large colonies. Mule's-Ears look similar but have much longer and narrower leaves. Seeds and thick taproots were eaten by Native Americans and early settlers.

Habitat: Open hills and sage communities
Life Zone: Foothills to montane
Flowering Time: Summer

Rocky Mountain Goldenrod
Solidago multiradiata
Sunflower Family - Asteraceae

This small perennial plant has dense, narrow clusters of blossoms on short stems. Individual flowers are composed of approximately 12 short rays, many disk flowers, and slender bracts in 3 tiers. Leaves are mostly basal and spoon-shaped and many stems grow from the tight cluster of leaves. Usually 10 inches tall, the plant can grow up to 20 inches tall.
Habitat: Open woods, meadows, and rocky areas
Life Zone: Foothills to subalpine
Flowering Time: Summer to fall

Alpine Avens
Geum rossii
(Syn: *Acomastylis rossii*)
Rose Family - Rosaceae

Bright yellow flowers with 5 rounded slightly notched petals often appear in dense clumps in alpine and sub-alpine meadows. Avens grow from 1 to 7 inches tall and are often found in soils disturbed by gophers and other alpine animals. Shiny fern-like basal leaves are from 1 to 8 inches long and form masses dotted with flowers. Leaves turn bronze to deep red in late summer.
Habitat: *Moist meadows, openings, and gravelly soils*
Life Zone: *Subalpine to alpine*
Flowering Time: *Summer to late summer*

Fragile Prickly Pear Cactus

Opuntia fragilis
Cactus Family - Cactaceae

This cactus spreads in mats up to several feet in diameter, but may lay flat or be only a few inches high. Delicate blossoms, up to 2 inches across, range from pale yellow to bronze. Pads or stems are shaped like a potato and have smooth surfaces with spines. Joints break easily (*fragilis*) and stick to animals that pass by. Prickly pears hybridize and are highly variable.

Habitat: *Sandy areas and in pinyon-juniper woodlands*
Life Zone: *Foothills to montane*
Flowering Time: *Spring to summer*

Sulphur Paintbrush

Alpine Paintbrush

Sulphur Paintbrush

(Yellow/ Northern Paintbrush)
Castilleja septentrionalis   (Syn: *C. sulphurea*)
Figwort Family - Scrophulariaceae

(APG: Broomrape Family - Orobanchaceae)

Sulphur Paintbrushes grow to 18 inches tall on leafy stems. Flowers are tiny greenish-yellow tubes surrounded by broad whitish-yellow lobed bracts. Inset: Shorter-growing (12 inches tall) Alpine Paintbrush, *Castilleja puberula,* is found above timberline. Its bracts and upper leaves are often cleft.
Habitat: *Meadows, open woods, and along streams*
Life Zone: *Montane to subalpine*
Flowering Time: *Early to late summer*

102

Golden Corydalis (Golden Smoke)
Corydalis aurea
Fumitory Family - Fumariaceae

This plant is one of the first to bloom in early summer. Low-growing herb grows from 3 to 12 inches high and can spread into a large clump. Bright yellow tubular flowers have 2 lips. Leaves are alternate and pinnately divided into fern-like linear segments. Although it looks similar to flowers in the pea family, Corydalis is in the Fumitory Family.

Habitat: Disturbed roadsides and gravelly soils
Life Zone: Foothills to Montane
Flowering Time: Early summer to early fall

Jeweled Blazingstar

Adonis Blazingstar

Jeweled Blazingstar
Mentzelia speciosa
Blazing Star Family - Loasaceae

These lovely plants grow to 2 feet tall and are difficult to identify. All species display some of the same unique qualities. Leaves, covered with stiff, hooked hairs, feel like sandpaper. Flowers are inconspicuous until they open in late afternoon or evening. *Mentzelia speciosa* has white to lemon outer petals and golden yellow inner petals. Inset: Adonis Blazingstar, *Mentzelia multiflora*, has all yellow petals.
Habitat: *Roadsides, gravelly soils, and grasslands*
Life Zone: *Foothills to montane*
Flowering Time: *Early to late summer*

Monkeyflower
Mimulus guttatus
Figwort Family - Scrophulariaceae

(APG III: Lopseed Family - Phrymaceae)

Monkeyflower grows from 4 to 15 inches high. Its delicate flowers consist of 2 upper petals and 3 lower petals fused together to form a tube or throat that is hairy with dark red spots inside. Leaves are opposite and oval-shaped with toothed edges. This native perennial appears as scattered plants or as masses of bright yellow blooms. Its sap can be used as a poultice for burns and skin irritations.
Habitat: In moist areas, inside and along streams
Life Zone: Foothills to subalpine
Flowering Time: Early to late summer

Alpine Sunflower (Old Man of the Mountain)
Hymenoxys grandiflora
(Syn: *Rydbergia grandiflora*)
Sunflower Family - Asteraceae

These distinctive, low-growing plants (up to 12 inches tall) have large, showy flower heads up to 4 inches across. Notched ray flowers surround a domed disk. Leaves are mostly basal and divided into narrow lobes. Leaves, stems, and bracts of the plant are all very woolly. This sunflower nearly always faces east.
Habitat: *On ridges, gravelly soils, and high meadows*
Life Zone: *Alpine*
Flowering Time: *Summer to late summer*

Blackeyed Susan
Rudbeckia hirta
Sunflower Family - Asteraceae

Blackeyed Susans are easy to spot with their large yellow to orange ray flowers with notched tips and blackish to light brown dome-shaped disks. Plants, up to 36 inches high, have rough, purplish hairy stems. Leaves are alternate, ovate with rounded teeth, up to 6 inches long and also hairy. Blackeyed Susans are popular in native gardens as they withstand drought.
Habitat: *Sunny areas in meadows and open woods*
Life Zone: *Foothills to montane*
Flowering Time: *Summer*

Blanketflower can be varicolored.

Blanketflower

(Gaillardia)
Gaillardia aristata
Sunflower Family - Asteraceae

Large flowerheads up to 3 1/2 inches across are composed of all yellow or yellow to reddish varicolored ray flowers around a large brown to maroon-colored raised disk. Blanket flowers have been used for dyes and medicinal purposes. Lance-shaped leaves and erect stems are hairy. Cultivated varieties are very popular.

Habitat: *Sunny hillsides, meadows, and open woods*
Life Zone: *Foothills to montane*
Flowering Time: *Summer to early fall*

False Dandelion
(Mountain Dandelion)
Agoseris glauca
Sunflower Family - Asteraceae

Large pale yellow flowerheads consist of strap-like ray flowers that resemble the common dandelion. The flowering stalk grows from 6 to 20 inches high and has milky juices. Pale green basal leaves vary from lance-shaped to small lobed and form an upright rosette.
Habitat: Dry meadows and grassy hillsides
Life Zone: Foothills to alpine
Flowering Time: Early summer to early fall

American Yellow-Rocket (Wintercress)
Barbarea orthoceras
Mustard Family - Brassicaceae

Wintercress grows from 1 to 2 feet tall and has round flower clusters of bright yellow blossoms. Individual flowers, up to 1/2 inch wide, have 4 petals (cruciform). Leaves are lobed, 2 to 6 inches long with rounded ends. Lower leaves are on stalks and upper leaves clasp the stem. This plant is toxic to animals.
Habitat: Moist areas, streamsides, and fields
Life Zone: Foothills to montane
Flowering Time: Spring to early fall

Avalanche-Lily (Glacier Lily)
Erythronium grandiflorum
Lily Family - Liliaceae

Glacier Lilies grows 12 inches tall and have one single blossom atop each stem. Nodding flowerheads consist of 6 tepals (no difference between petals and sepals) curving backwards and 6 noticeable stamens facing downward. Shiny green leaves are mostly basal. Glacier Lilies often appear in patches as the snow melts and are one of the first flowers to bloom.
Habitat: *Melting snowbanks, along streams, meadows*
Life Zone: *Foothills to alpine*
Flowering Time: *Late spring to early summer*

Sneezeweed (Orange Sneezeweed)
Hymenoxys hoopseii
(Synonym: *Dugaldia hoopseii*)
Sunflower Family - Asteraceae

Sneezeweed is easily identified by its yellow-orange color and its long, drooping ray flowers (up to 1 inch long) surrounding a mound-shaped orange disk (up to 1 inch across). Leaves are lance-shaped, 5 to 10 inches at the base of the plant and smaller toward the top. White mid-veins are evident in leaves.
Habitat: Meadows and open woods
Life Zone: Montane to subalpine
Flowering Time: Summer to early fall

Tall Coneflower

(Goldenglow, Cutleaf Coneflower)
Rudbeckia laciniata
(Synonym: *Rudbeckia ampla*)
Sunflower Family - Asteraceae

This stately plant grows up to 6 feet tall and has large yellow flowerheads up to 5 inches across. Drooping ray flowers surround a yellow-green cone-shaped disk. As the disk flowers are pollinated, they turn yellow to brown. Leaves are alternate, long and wide, and are deeply lobed or cut into toothed-edged segments.
Habitat: Streamsides and moist soils
Life Zone: Foothills to montane
Flowering Time: Summer to early fall

Mule's-Ears
Wyethia amplexicaulis
Sunflower Family - Asteraceae

Mule's-Ears derives its name from the size and shape of the large, shiny and upright basal leaves (from 4 to 16 inches long). Stems leaves are smaller and clasp the stem. Plants grow up to 3 feet tall and can cover huge expanses of meadows and hillsides. Flowerheads, 3 to 5 inches across, have both ray and disk flowers.
Habitat: *Meadows and hillsides*
Life Zone: *Foothills to montane*
Flowering Time: *Early summer to summer*

Nodding Sunflower

(Five-nerved Aspen Sunflower)
Helianthella quinquenervis
Sunflower Family - Asteraceae

This tall sunflower, up to 4 feet tall, has one large nodding flowerhead 3 to 4 inches across per stem. Lemon yellow ray flowers surround a darker yellow disk. Leaves, oval to elliptical, are leathery and up to a foot long at the base of the plant; there are few stem leaves. Most leaves have 5 prominent veins.
Habitat: *Forest openings, aspen groves, meadows*
Life Zone: *Montane to subalpine*
Flowering Time: *Summer*

Photo © Courtesy of Al Schneider

Yellow Lady's Slipper
Cypripedium parviflorum var. pubescens
(Syn: *Cypripedium calceolus*)
Orchid Family - Orchidaceae

Yellow Lady's Slipper is rare and should be admired only with one's eyes or a camera lens. Its spectacular fragrant blossom is up to 2 inches long and has 3 twisted tan sepals, 2 similar petals and a third bright yellow shoe-shaped petal with red to purple spots inside. Large, wide leaves, up to 6 inch long, are alternate.

Habitat: In moist areas and forest clearings
Life Zone: Foothills to subalpine
Flowering Time: Summer

Yellow Pond-Lily

(Rocky Mountain Pond-Lily)
Nuphar polysepala   (Synonym: *Nuphar lutea*)
Waterlily Family - Nymphaeaceae

This aquatic plant has large floating, round to heart-shaped leathery leaves up to 16 inches long. Yellow cup-shaped flowers consist of 6 to 9 waxy petal-like sepals encircling the petals along with reddish-purple stamens and a lobed stigma. This native plant provides a habitat for many aquatic animals.
Habitat: Ponds, small lakes, and tarns
Life Zone: Foothills to subalpine
Flowering Time: Early to late summer

117

Alpine Thistle
(Dragonhead Thistle, Frostyball)
Cirsium scopulorum
Sunflower Family - Asteraceae

This thistle is easily identified by its giant, nodding flowerheads. Flower color ranges from yellow to purple, but the the blossoms are usually hidden with a covering of woolly hair. Plants grow to 3 feet tall making them giants among alpine flowers. Leaves are wavy, up to 6 inches long, toothed and tipped with 1/2 inch spines.
Habitat: *Rocky slopes and meadows*
Life Zone: *Subalpine to alpine*
Flowering Time: *Summer to early fall*

Butter and Eggs
Linaria vulgaris
Figwort Family-
Scrophulariaceae

(APG III: Plantain Family - Plantaginaceae)

Although attractive with snapdragon-like yellow flowers, Butter and Eggs is a non-native invasive plant. Blossoms, up to an inch long, have 2 lips, an orange spot on the lower lip, and a long spur at its base. Flowers form a spike atop erect stems. Leaves are alternate, narrow, and gray-green color. Plant emits an unpleasant odor.
Habitat: Roadsides and disturbed open areas
Life Zone: Foothills to montane
Flowering Time: Summer to fall

119

Subalpine Buttercup
Ranunculus eschscholtzii
Buttercup Family - Raunculaceae

Bright yellow flowers, approximately 1 inch across, have 5 to 12 waxy rounded petals with numerous prominent stamens. There are 5 green to brown or purple sepals. Plants are low growing, 2 to 10 inches high, but are often found in large patches. Lower leaves are wide and lobed or in 3 parts with stems. Upper leaves are similar, smaller, and sometimes clasp the flower stem.
Habitat: By melting snow, wet areas, and streambanks
Life Zone: Subalpine to alpine
Flowering Time: Early to late summer

Goat's-Beard

(Yellow Salsify)
Tragopogon dubius
Sunflower Family - Asteraceae

This non-native dandelion look-alike grows up to 3 feet tall and has a flowerhead composed of many ray flowers. Its green bracts extend well beyond the flowerhead. Leaves are grass-like, alternately attached and clasp the stem. Every part of the plant produces a milky sap. Giant ball-shaped seed head, up to 4 inches in diameter, resembles an old gray goat's beard.

Habitat: *Dry places, along roadsides, and open fields*
Life Zone: *Foothills to montane*
Flowering Time: *Summer*

121

Dwarf Golden Aster

Heterotheca pumila
Sunflower Family - Asteraceae

Plants (5 to 10 inches tall) grow in circular mounds. Flowerheads, up to 1 1/4 inches across have bright yellow ray flowers surrounding a 3/8 inch orange disk. Leaves, with spoon-shaped blades, crowd near the top of the stem. Lower leaves wither early but remain on the plant. Stems, usually with a single flower, are reddish, woolly, and woody.

Habitat: *On ridges, gravelly soils, and high meadows*
Life Zone: *Subalpine to alpine*
Flowering Time: *Summer to late summer*

Curly-cup Gumweed
Grindelia squarrosa
Sunflower Family - Asteraceae

Curly-cup Gumweed grows into a shrubby plant 8 to 24 inches tall. Each plant has many flowerheads consisting of short ray flowers around a darker center disk. Its most notable features besides its sticky, resinous nature are the rounded backward-curling bracts below the flowers. Leaves are oblong and toothed and sometimes have resin dots.

Habitat: Dry soils and open slopes
Life Zone: Foothills
Flowering Time: Summer to early fall

Nodding Groundsel (Rayless Senecio)
Senecio bigelovii (Syn: *Ligularia bigelovii*)
Sunflower Family - Asteraceae

Small, nodding flowerheads consist of only disk flowers enclosed by green to purplish bracts. Plants grow from 1 to 3 feet tall with stems that often branch near the top. Base leaves are lance-shaped to oblong and toothed. Upper leaves are smaller and clasp the stem. The plant appears as if the flowers have not yet opened.
Habitat: Forests and meadows
Life Zone: Montane to subalpine
Flowering Time: Summer to early fall

Broadleaf Arnica
Arnica latifolia
Sunflower Family - Asteraceae

Bright yellow flowerheads, up to 1 1/2 inches across, have notched ray flowers (8 to 12 rays) and darker disk flowers. Bracts are long, hairy and pointed. Leaves are oval to triangular-shaped and attached in 5 to 9 opposite pairs. Erect stems have 1 to 5 flowerheads up to 1 1/2 inches across. Plants grow up to 16 inches tall. The plant is highly toxic if ingested.

Habitat: Shady woodlands and moist areas
Life Zone: Montane to alpine
Flowering Time: Summer to early fall

125

Prairie Coneflower
(Mexican Hat)
Ratibida columnifera
Sunflower Family - Asteraceae

Flowerheads have a distinctive finger-like yellow to brown cone-shaped disk surrounded by ray flowers facing downward. Ray flowers vary from yellow to dark red. Leaves are hairy, alternate, and deeply lobed into 5 to 9 parts. Plants sometimes grow in large groups and reach heights from 1 to 3 feet tall.

Habitat: Sunny slopes and along roadsides
Life Zone: Foothills
Flowering Time: Summer to early fall

Goldeneye
Heliomeris multiflora
(Synonym: *Viguiera multiflora*)
Sunflower Family - Asteraceae

Showy sunflowers form bushy plants with many flowers on slender stems. Slightly notched ray flowers surround a gold-yellow domed disk. Leaves are grayish green, lance-shaped, toothed and feel like sandpaper. Bristly stems are from 2 to 4 feet tall and branched many times. Plants are showy and bloom for many weeks.
Habitat: Roadsides, dry soils, and hillsides
Life Zone: Foothills to subalpine
Flowering Time: Summer to late summer

127

Leafy Cinquefoil

(Big-flowered Cinquefoil)

Drymocallis fissa   (Synonym: *Potentilla fissa*)
Rose Family - Rosaceae

Light yellow 5-petalled flowers, up to 1 inch across, resemble buttercups. Blossoms are in clusters on leafy stems up to 12 inches tall. Sharply-toothed leaves are compound with 9 to 13 broad leaflets. Both stems and foliage have brown sticky hairs. This low-growing plant, like other cinquefoils, has medicinal qualities.

Habitat: Rocky slopes, trailsides, and forest clearings
Life Zone: Foothills to montane
Flowering Time: Late spring to late summer

Shrubby Cinquefoil
Dasiphora fruticosa
(Synonym: *Potentilla fruticosa*)
Rose Family - Rosaceae

Shrubby Cinquefoil with long-lasting blooms, forms a rounded, leafy shrub that grows from 1 to 5 feet high. Bright yellow flowers are saucer-shaped, up to 1 1/2 inches wide, and have 5 petals and 5 sepal-like bracts. Small leaves are alternate and pinnately compound, divided with 3 to 7 narrow leaflets.

Habitat: Meadows, shrublands, and open hillsides
Life Zone: Foothills to subalpine
Flowering Time: Early summer to early fall

Yellow Stonecrop (Lanceleaf Stonecrop)
Sedum lanceolatum
(Synonym: *Amerosedum lanceolatum*)
Stonecrop Family - Crassulaceae

These distinctive, bright yellow star-shaped flowers grow close to the ground on short, succulent stems, up to 5 inches high. Flowers consist of 5 petals, 5 sepals and protruding stamens. Small, fleshy leaves, are alternate and have blunt tips. Basal leaves can be green to reddish brown.
Habitat: *Gravelly slopes and roadsides*
Life Zone: *Foothills to alpine*
Flowering Time: *Summer to early fall*

Western Wallflower
Erysimum capitatum
Mustard Family - Brassicaceae

Wallflowers are highly variable with flowers that can range in color from yellow to orange or even maroon or lavender. Plants grow from 8 to 20 inches high with flowers in rounded, showy clusters. Blossoms have 4 petals and are 1/2 to 3/4 inches across. Grayish-green leaves are linear and mostly basal.

Habitat: Forest opening, along ridges, and meadows
Life Zone: Foothills to alpine
Flowering Time: Spring to late summer

131

Mountain Goldenbanner

Thermopsis montana
Pea Family - Fabaceae

Showy yellow flowers grow to 3 feet tall. Blossoms, similar to lupine, are formed in loose clusters at top of stems. Leaves are alternate and compound, divided into 3 leaflets. Goldenbanner often grows in large colonies in spring. Fruits are flat, curved pea pods. Goldenbanner is native, common and widespread.

Habitat: *Mountain meadows and roadsides*
Life Zone: *Foothills to montane*
Flowering Time: *Spring to early summer*

Snow Buttercup (Alpine Buttercup)
Ranunculus adoneus
Buttercup Family - Ranunculaceae

Flowers, up to 1 1/2 inches across, are glossy yellow with 5 to 12 overlapping petals, and 5 hairy sepals that can be green or purplish. Plants grow to 12 inches tall and are often found by snowbanks. Leaves are deeply cut into narrow lobes. Basal leaves are about two inches long and wide.

Habitat: Wet areas near snow and streamsides
Life Zone: Subalpine to alpine
Flowering Time: Early summer to late summer

133

Mountain Parsley

Cymopteris lemmonii
(Syn: *Pseudocymopterus montanus*)
Parsley Family - Apiaceae

Tiny yellow flowers form flat-topped to rounded umbrella-like clusters approximately 2 inches wide. Leaves, on long stalks, are smooth, dark green and divided into fine cut fern-like leaflets that smell and look similar to flat-leaf parsley sold in markets. Plants grow from 3 to 18" tall.
Habitat: *Woodlands, meadows, and rocky slopes*
Life Zone: *Foothills to alpine*
Flowering Time: *Late spring to late summer*

Golden Draba
Draba aurea
Mustard Family -
Brassicaceae

Bright yellow flowers are clustered on hairy, erect stems up to 10 inches tall. Flowers have of 4 petals, 4 tall stamens, 2 short stamens, and 4 hairy sepals. Leaves are thick, oval to spoon-shaped and hairy along stem and at the base of the plant. Golden Draba plants often appear grey-green because of their hairy stems and leaves.
Habitat: Open woods and meadows
Life Zone: Montane to alpine
Flowering Time: Summer

135

Common Mullein
Verbascum thapsus
Figwort Family - Scrophulariaceae

Tall biennial plants (14 to 60 inches) have long spikes of bright saucer-shaped yellow flowers. Basal rosette leaves and stem leaves are large, lance-shaped, soft, and fuzzy. Plant is a non-native, noxious weed.
Habitat: *Sandy soils, roadsides, and disturbed areas*
Life Zone: *Foothills to montane*
Flowering Time: *Summer to late summer*

Western Golden Ragwort
Senecio eremophilus
Sunflower Family - Asteraceae

Tall erect plant grows from 12 to 36 inches high and has numerous bright yellow flowers in a cluster per stem. Small flowerheads have 7 to 10 ray flowers around center disks. Deeply cut lobed leaves are lobed or toothed; lower leaves are stalked.
Habitat: *Rocky areas, meadows, and roadsides*
Life Zone: *Montane to subalpine*
Flowering Time: *Summer*

137

Parry's Lousewort
Pedicularis parryi
Figwort Family - Scrophulariaceae

(APG III: Broomrape Family - Orobanchaceae)

Plants with erect, smooth stems grow to 16 inches tall. Flowers form a spike of white to yellowish blossoms up to 3/4 of an inch across. Upper lip of the flower is beak-shaped and flower stalks have purple streaks. Leaves are mostly basal and are pinnately divided into narrow lobes similar to leaves of Elephantheads.

Habitat: *Dry meadows and hillsides*
Life Zone: *Subalpine to alpine*
Flowering Time: *Summer to late summer*

Fernleaf Lousewort

Towering Lousewort

Fernleaf Lousewort (Bracted Lousewort)
Pedicularis bracteosa
Figwort Family - Scrophulariaceae

(APG III: Broomrape Family - Orobanchaceae)

This plant grows up to 3 feet tall and has a large spike of pale yellow flowers atop a coarse, hairy, unbranched stem. Flowers have upper lips that are beak-like and lower lips with 3 lobes. Leaves are alternate, fern-like with toothed margins. Inset: Towering or giant Lousewort, *pedicularis procera*, has red-streaked flowers.
Habitat: *Forests, meadows, and open slopes*
Life Zone: *Subalpine*
Flowering Time: *Summer*

139

Daffodil Senecio
Senecio amplectens
(Syn: *Ligularia amplectens*)
Sunflower Family - Asteraceae

Large, bright lemon yellow flowers with pointed tips nod atop almost leafless stems. Wide bracts surrounding the flowerheads can become dark purple-brown. Plants grow from 8 to 24 inches tall and often appear in small patches. Leaves are mostly basal and can be smooth or have rounded margins.
Habitat: *Woodlands, mountainsides, and meadows*
Life Zone: *Montane to subalpine*
Flowering Time: *Summer to fall*

Mountain Gumweed
Grindelia subalpina
Sunflower Family - Asteraceae

Flowers, 1 to 1 1/2 inches across, have yellow rays and
centers and sticky, sometimes reddish bracts that curl
backwards and downwards. Petals also sometimes curl
with age. Plants have many branches and grow from 8
to 18 inches tall. Leaves are alternate, thick, to 3 inches
long, and are sharply toothed to lobed.
Habitat: Dry open areas, roadsides, and on slopes
Life Zone: Montane to subalpine
Flowering Time: Summer to fall

141

Heartleaf Arnica
Arnica cordifolia
Sunflower Family - Asteraceae

Plants grow from 5 to 24 inches high and have single stems with 2 to 4 pairs of opposite, mostly heart-shaped leaves with toothed margins. Lower leaves are larger and on stalks. Flowerheads have golden yellow disk flowers surrounded by 9 to 15 bright lemon color ray flowers. Bracts have long hairs and are pointed.
Habitat: *Shaded areas and open woods*
Life Zone: *Montane to subalpine*
Flowering Time: *Summer to late summer*

Arrowleaf Groundsel

(Arrowleaf Ragwort)
Senecio triangularis
Sunflower Family - Asteraceae

This large plant can grow up to 5 feet tall and has a loose cluster of yellow blossoms each up to 1 inch wide. Ray flowers (6 to 12) form around a small darker yellow to orange disk. Leaves are triangular with sharply toothed edges and are up to 8 inches long. Plants sometimes grow in large clumps along streamsides.
Habitat: Moist areas in meadows and near streams
Life Zone: Montane
Flowering Time: Summer to fall

Rubber Rabbitbrush
Ericameria nauseosa
(Syn: *Chrysothamnus nauseosus*)
Sunflower Family - Asteraceae

This native shrub can grow up to 6 feet tall. Its yellow disk flowers form large, round clusters 1 to 4 inches across. Leaves are alternate, narrow, 1 to 3 inches long and gray-green. Plant leaves and flexible twigs are covered with felt-like hairs. Rabbitbrush is common and highly variable. It attracts all kinds of insect pollinators.
Habitat: Dry open sites and along roadsides
Life Zone: Foothills to montane
Flowering Time: Late summer to fall

Orange Agoseris

(Burnt Orange Dandelion)
Agoseris aurantiaca
Sunflower Family - Asteraceae

Solitary flowers grow on leafless stems from 5 to 24 inches tall. Orange to orange-red colored blossoms consist of only ray flowers and the outer petals have squared tips with small teeth. Leaves are on long stalks and form a basal rosette. Flowers resemble dandelions and produce a milky sap.
Habitat: Woodlands, grassy meadows, and slopes
Life Zone: Foothills to subalpine
Flowering Time: Summer to late summer

145

Field Mint (Wild Mint)
Mentha arvensis
Mint Family - Lamiaceae

Field Mint grows up to 3 feet tall and has a distinctive mint-like smell. Tiny white to pink flowers are clustered in leaf axils along the upper part of the square stem. Individual flowers have a notched upper lip and a 3-lobed lower lip and protruding stamens. Leaves are opposite with pointed tips and sharp teeth.
Habitat: *Moist areas along ditches, and streamsides*
Life Zone: *Foothills to montane*
Flowering Time: *Summer to fall*

Firecracker Penstemon (Scarlet Bugler)
Penstemon barbatus
Figwort Family - Scrophulariaceae

(APG III: Plantain Family - Plantaginaceae)

Tall plant, up to 3 feet high, has an unbranched red stem
with nodes several inches apart. Flowers are scattered
along stem in racemes up to 8 inches long. Brilliant red
flowers, up to 2 inches long, are tubular with an over-
hanging upper lip and a drooping lower lip. Upper leaves
are linear and basal leaves are more spoon-shaped.
Habitat: *Rocky canyonsides and gravelly soils*
Life Zone: *Foothills*
Flowering Time: *Summer*

147

Bog Saxifrage

(Oregon Saxifrage)
Micranthes oregana
Saxifrage Family - Saxifragaceae

Bog Saxifrage grows up to 12 inches tall with a thick, erect, hairy, and sticky stem. Tiny white to reddish flowers form in clusters along the stem and are characterized by 5 oval petals and 5 reflexed sepals. Leaves are basal and fleshy with small teeth. Fruit is pear-shaped and reddish.

Habitat: Wet meadows and streamsides
Life Zone: Subalpine to alpine
Flowering Time: Summer

148

Pink Pyrola

(Pink Wintergreen)
Pyrola asarifolia
(Synonym: *Pyrola rotundifolia*)
Wintergreen Family - Pyrolaceae

(APG III: Heath Family - Ericaceae)

Pink cup-shaped nodding flowers are arranged in racemes on slender, smooth stems from 4 to 12 inches tall. Round to elliptical leaves with rounded teeth, form a basal rosette. "Pyrola" is derived from "Pyrus" that means pear tree, as the leaves resemble pear leaves.
Habitat: *Wet areas, bogs and willow thickets*
Life Zone: *Montane to subalpine*
Flowering Time: *Summer*

149

Redstem Fillaree
(Storkbill)
Erodium cicutarium
Geranium Family - Geraniaceae

This plant grows up to 8 inches tall with tiny purplish-pink showy flowers that bloom in clusters of two or more. Fern-like opposite leaves and reddish stems are hairy. Fruit resembles a stork's bill. This exotic species, introduced by the Spanish in the early 1700s, is considered a noxious weed in Colorado.

Habitat: *Dry pasturelands, roadsides, and sandy soils*
Life Zone: *Foothills to montane*
Flowering Time: *Early spring to late fall*

Alpine Clover

Parry's Clover

Alpine Clover

(Rose Clover)
Trifolium dasyphyllum
Pea Family - Fabaceae

Alpine Clover grows up to 5 inches tall and is often forms small cushions. Flowers are two-toned white and purplish pink, 1/2 of an inch across. Leaves are basal, long-stalked, and divided into 3 narrow, pointed leaflets. Inset: Parry's Clover, *Trifolium parryi,* is somewhat larger and has pink, reddish to purplish flowerheads.
Habitat: Along streams, meadows, and gravelly slopes
Life Zone: Subalpine to alpine
Flowering Time: Summer to late summer

151

Moss Campion (Moss Pink)
Silene acaulis
Pink Family - Caryophyllaceae

This native perennial forms large, dense, moss-like mats up to 10 inches in diameter. Tiny, tubular pink to white flowers grow singly on stems to 2 inches high and have 5 reflexed notched petals. Leaves are basal, bright green, linear, and up to 1 1/2 inches long. Moss Campion often grows near Alpine Forget-Me-Nots.

Habitat: Rocky soils, hillsides, and rock crevices
Life Zone: Alpine
Flowering Time: Summer

Wood Lily
(Rocky Mountain Lily, Red Lily)
Lilium philadelphicum
Lily Family - Liliaceae

This beautiful lily is rare and endangered in many areas of Colorado. Its unmistakable orange to bright red flowers are up to 2 1/2 inches across and consist of 6 tepals (sepals and petals look the same) and purple anthers. Petals and sepals are spotted at the base. Plant grows to 2 feet tall and has alternate lower leaves and whorled upper leaves.

Habitat: Open woods and moist meadows
Life Zone: Foothills to montane
Flowering Time: Summer

Red Columbine (Shooting Star Columbine)
Aquilegia elegantula
Buttercup Family - Ranunculaceae

Nodding red and yellow flowers, 1 to 2 inches across, consist of 5 red petals with thin spurs pointing backwards, 5 rounded sepals and numerous yellow stamens. Plants, from 6 to 18 inches tall, are found mainly west of the Continental Divide. Basal and stem leaves are compound and cut into leaflets with rounded lobes. Plant seeds and roots are very toxic if consumed.

Habitat: Moist soils of forest edges and openings
Life Zone: Montane to subalpine
Flowering Time: Summer

Scarlet Gilia (Skyrocket)
Ipomopsis aggregata
(Synonym: *Gilia aggregata*)
Phlox Family - Polemoniaceae

Delicate flowers are long, fused tubes with 5 pointed petals pointing backwards. Trumpet-shaped flowers, arranged in loose clusters, can be pink, salmon-colored, red or even white. Plants are to 3 feet tall, have finely cut, hairy leaves that are attached alternately. Stems and leaves smell "skunky" when crushed.
Habitat: Gravelly soils, dry meadows, and open areas
Life Zone: Foothills to montane
Flowering Time: Spring to fall

Rose Crown (Queen's Crown)
Rhodiola rhodantha
(Synonym: *Clementsia rhodantha*)
Stonecrop Family - Crassulaceae

Rose Crown flowers are terminal pink clusters resembling clover atop succulent looking plants. Flower color may vary from white to rose pink. Fleshy and linear leaves thickly cover the entire stem from top to bottom. Plants grow to 14 inches tall and form dense colonies. In fall, leaves turn from green to red.

Habitat: *Wet meadows and near streams*
Life Zone: *Subalpine to alpine*
Flowering Time: *Summer to fall*

King's Crown (Roseroot, Western Roseroot)
Rhodiola integrifolia
(Synonym: *Sedum roseum*)
Stonecrop Family - Crassulaceae

Succulent plants grow from 4 to 12 inches tall and are topped with tiny dark red to maroon flowers in a tight flat-topped cluster. Stamens with purple filaments extend beyond the petals. Leaves and stems are fleshy, and like Rose Crown, turn shades of yellow, green, red and orange in fall.
Habitat: Moist and dry meadows and woodlands
Life Zone: Subalpine to alpine
Flowering Time: Summer to fall

Wyoming Paintbrush
Castilleja linariifolia
Figwort Family - Scrophulariaceae
(APG III: Broomrape Family - Orobanchaceae)

Flowers are a cluster of tubular green-yellow petals and red to orange-colored bracts that are split part way. Plants grow to 3 feet tall and have branched stems. Leaves are very narrow and entire or sometimes lobed. This Paintbrush grows at lower elevations and is the state flower of Wyoming.
Habitat: Meadows, forest openings, shrublands
Life Zone: Foothills to montane
Flowering Time: Summer

Dwarf Clover (Deer Clover)
Trifolium nanum
Pea Family - Fabaceae

Low-growing clover has only 1 to 4 pea-shaped blossoms per head. Colors can range from white to light or dark pink. Sharply pointed leaves, 3 to a stem, form mats that are usually no more than 2 inches high. Although there are fewer flowers than leaves, the blossoms appear large (up to 1 inch long) in comparison to the rest of the plant.

Habitat: Meadows and gravelly soils
Life Zone: Subalpine to alpine
Flowering Time: Early to midsummer

Wild Bergamot

(Horsemint, Beebalm)
Monarda fistulosa
Mint Family - Lamiaceae

Rose to purplish flowers (white are rare) form in shaggy clusters above leafy bracts. Individual blossoms are tubular with a narrow upper lip and a 3-lobed lower lip. Lance-shaped, sharply toothed fragrant leaves are opposite along square, unbranched stems. Native people used the leaves to make tea to treat ailments.
Habitat: Moist soils in open woods and meadows
Life Zone: Foothills to montane
Flowering Time: Summer

Rocky Mountain
Beeplant (Spiderflower)
Peritoma serrulata (Synonym: *Cleome serrulata*)
Caper Family - Capparaceae
(APG III: Cleome Family - Cleomaceae)

This showy plant has a large round cluster of pink to purplish flowers (white is rare) from 2 to 4 inches across. Each flower has 4 fused petals with 6 long stamens extending beyond the petals. Leaves are alternate and divided into 3 lance-shaped leaflets on short stalks. Seed pods taper at both ends and often appear along with new blossoms.
Habitat: Roadsides and dry disturbed soils
Life Zone: Foothills to montane
Flowering Time: Late spring to summer

161

Strawberry Blite
Chenopodium capitatum
Goosefoot Family - Chenopodiaceae

(APG III: Amaranth Family - Amaranthaceae)

Strawberry Blite or Blite Goosefoot is an edible annual plant. Strawberry-like clusters of rounded, dense flowers form a spike on erect stems 4 to 16 inches tall. Leaves are triangular and coarsely toothed. The entire plant turns red as it matures. Young leaves can be used as potherb and the fruit clusters can be eaten raw.
Habitat: *Roadsides, shady woods, and moist valleys*
Life Zone: *Foothills to montane*
Flowering Time: *Early to late summer*

Rose Gentian

(Little Gentian, Northern Gentian)
Gentianella amarella   (Syn: *Gentianella acuta*)
Gentian Family - Gentianaceae

Tiny pale pink to blue to lavender flowers grow 2 to 15 inches tall on slender, curved, leafy stems. Blossoms form in clusters in upper leaf axils. Each blossom is tubular with 4 pointed lobes and a hairy fringed throat. Leaves are opposite and up to 1 1/2 inches long. Gentian plants are traditionally used to treat digestive ailments.
Habitat: Moist meadows, willow thickets, woodlands
Life Zone: Montane to subalpine
Flowering Time: Summer to fall

Canada Thistle
Cirsium arvense
Sunflower Family - Asteraceae

Canada Thistle is a non-native, invasive plant often found in large groupings. Pink to purple flowerheads are composed of only disk flowers encased in prickly green bracts with hooked ends. Leaves are irregularly lobed and have sharp spines on the lobe tips. Stems are branched and spineless reaching heights of 1 to 5 feet. This thistle is on the Colorado noxious weed list.
Habitat: Fields, roadsides, and disturbed areas
Life Zone: Foothills to montane
Flowering Time: Summer

Musk Thistle
(Nodding Thistle)
Carduus nutans
Sunflower Family - Asteraceae

This non-native thistle can grow from 3 to 6 feet tall. Large pink to light purple nodding flowerheads are up to 3 inches across and composed of only disk flowers. Bracts are triangular, tipped with spines and sometimes curved backwards. Leaves are lance-shaped and lobed with serrated edges and white spines. Musk Thistle is considered a noxious weed in Colorado.
Habitat: Overgrazed meadows and roadsides
Life Zone: Foothills to montane
Flowering Time: Summer to early fall

165

Rocky Mountain Clover

(Weak Clover)
Trifolium attenuatum
Pea Family - Fabaceae

This clover often forms large, sprawling circular mats. Flowerheads composed of small, elongated pea-like flowers have a shaggy appearance and droop to the ground with their weight. Trifold, narrow leaves are on long stalks and are often folded. Plants grow to 6 inches high, but their mats can be several feet in diameter.

Habitat: *Gravelly meadows and sandy, rocky soil*
Life Zone: *Subalpine to alpine*
Flowering Time: *Summer*

Cutleaf Anemone
(Red Windflower)
Anemone multifida
Buttercup Family - Ranunculaceae

Unique plant, 8 to 20 inches high, has 1 to 3 hairy stems topped with single flowers. Flowers have 5 to 9 petal-like sepals hairy at tips that vary in color from cream to yellow to red or combinations of colors. Leaves are divided into pointed lobes and cluster at the base of the plant. Smaller leaves whorl around the middle of the stems.
Habitat: Fields, open woods, and disturbed areas
Life Zone: Montane to alpine
Flowering Time: Summer

167

Geyer Onion (Wild Onion)
Allium geyeri
Lily Family - Liliaceae

(APG III: Onion Family - Alliaceae)

Geyer Onion grows to 20 inches tall except above timberline where it grows as a dwarf variety. Small clustered pink to lavender flowers grow on a stout stem. Individual blossoms are approximately 1/4 inch with pointed petals and papery bracts. Slender long leaves are folded and have a characteristic onion odor.

Habitat: Meadows and forest openings
Life Zone: Montane to alpine
Flowering Time: Summer

American Vetch (Wild Pea)
Vicia americana
Pea Family - Fabaceae

American Vetch is a slender vine with tendrils that attach
to surrounding plants or objects. Its purple to reddish
flowers are attached in loose clusters on stalks at the leaf
axils. Leaves are alternate and pinnately compound with
8 to 18 oblong leaflets and a tendril replacing the top
leaflet. Plants grow up to 30 inches long.
Habitat: Meadows, grassy slopes, along roadsides
Life Zone: Foothills to montane
Flowering Time: Summer

169

Red Paintbrush (Common Paintbrush)
Castilleja miniata
Figwort Family - Scrophulariaceae
(APG III: Broomrape Family - Orobanchaceae)

Bright red lobed bracts in a dense cluster almost hide the 2-lipped tubular green flowers. Plants, up to 3 feet tall, have numerous hairy, sticky stems. Leaves are lance-shaped, alternate and entire with some upper leaves lobed. Red Paintbrush may appear red, salmon and pink as it often hybridizes with other paintbrushes.
Habitat: Forest openings, along streams, meadows
Life Zone: Foothills to subalpine
Flowering Time: Late spring to fall

Rosy Paintbrush
Castilleja rhexiifolia
Figwort Family - Scrophulariaceae
(APG III: Broomrape Family - Orobanchaceae)

Flowers are inconspicuous narrow green tubes enclosed by rosy pink bracts. Plants are up to 20 inches high. Lance-shaped narrow leaves have 3 noticeable veins. Paintbrushes are semi-parasitic and derive nutrients from other host plants. Rosy Paintbrush hybridizes with Sulphur Paintbrush and has many color variations.
Habitat: Dry slopes and meadows
Life Zone: Subalpine to alpine
Flowering Time: Summer

Marsh Dock
(Dense-flowered Dock)
Rumex densiflorus
Buckwheat Family - Polygonaceae

These plants grow to 3 or more feet tall and are characterized by small, densely-clustered flowers in huge flowerheads. Large oblong leaves are up to 15 inches long with conspicuous veins. Plants are more noticeable when flowers turn to red and green seeds.
Habitat: *Wetlands, streamsides, and moist meadows*
Life Zone: *Montane to alpine*
Flowering Time: *Summer*

Horsemint
(Nettleleaf Giant Hyssop)
Agastache urticifolia
Mint Family - Lamiaceae

Giant Hyssop grows from 1 to 4 feet tall and has a 4-sided stem and aromatic, musky leaves. White to purple small trumpet-shaped flowers form a noticeable spike. Each small flower has a stigma and 4 stamen that extend outward from the flower's throat. Leaves are arrow-shaped and opposite and are forage for wildlife.
Habitat: Mountain meadows and open sites
Life Zone: Montane to alpine
Flowering Time: Summer

173

Red Clover

White Clover

Red Clover
Trifolium pratense
Pea Family - Fabaceae

Red clover is a non-native plant introduced in the 1800s as a pasture crop. It grows from 6 to 20 inches high with rose-red flowerheads composed of many small, narrow flowers. Leaves, on stalks, are divided into 3 variegated leaflets. Trifoliate bracts extend below the flowerheads. Inset: White Clover, *Trifolium repens* is smaller, low growing, and has more rounded leaflets
Habitat: *Roadsides, fields, and disturbed areas*
Life Zone: *Plains to montane*
Flowering Time: *Spring through fall*

Alpine Lousewort
Pedicularis scopulorum (Syn: *Pedicularis sudetica*)
Figwort Family - Scrophulariaceae

(APG III: Broomrape Family - Orobanchaceae)

Alpine Lousewort grows almost exclusively in the Colorado Rockies. This unique plant has rose to slight purple-colored beak-like flowers in crowded spikes on short stems, 4 to 8 inches tall. Spiked flowerheads are quite hairy. Basal leaves of the plant are lance-shaped and divided like a comb almost to mid-rib.
Habitat: Moist meadows and lake shores
Life Zone: Subalpine to alpine
Flowering Time: Summer

Pygmy Bitterroot (Alpine Lewisia)
Lewisia pygmaea　　(Synonym: *Lewisia minima*)
Purslane Family - Portulacaceae
(APG III: Miner's Lettuce Family - Montiaceae)

Small pink to rose or sometimes white flowers, 1/2 inch across, are on low-growing succulent plants. Flowers consist of 5 to 8 petals surrounding star-shaped pistils. Fleshy leaves are flattened and linear forming a basal rosette. Plants grow up to 4 inches tall. Native people gathered the carrot-like roots as a food source.
Habitat: Meadows and gravelly soils
Life Zone: Montane to alpine
Flowering Time: Early summer to summer

Narrowleaf Collomia (Tiny Trumpet)
Collomia linearis
Phlox Family - Polemoniaceae

Tiny pale pink trumpet-shaped flowers, 1/4 inch across, grow in a cluster in the upper leaf axils. Slender, leafy plant is from 4 to 12 inches tall and has a hairy erect stem. Leaves are linear to lance-shaped, alternate and are larger toward the top of the plant. Collomia is quite common and found in all Western states.

Habitat: Roadsides, grasslands, and disturbed areas
Life Zone: Foothills to montane
Flowering Time: Late spring to summer

Fairy Primrose (Alpine Primrose)
Primula angustifolia
Primrose Family - Primulaceae

Although only 2 to 3 inches tall, these miniature plants have showy bright pink to rose-colored flowers that appear just above mounds of fleshy leaves close to the ground. Fragrant flowers have 5 notched petals surrounding yellow centers. Leaves, 2 inches long, are narrow and often folded.
Habitat: Boulder fields, rock crevices, and rocky soils
Life Zone: Subalpine to alpine
Flowering Time: Summer

Alpine Fireweed (Dwarf Fireweed)
Chamerion latifolium
(Syn: *Chamerion subdentatum*)
Evening Primrose Family - Onagraceae

Alpine Fireweed grows to 16 inches tall with reddish purple leaning stems. Flowers have 1 inch pink to purple petals and extended stamens. Leaves are opposite and oval to elliptical with sometimes finely toothed edges. This plant is similar to the common fireweed but is short, has fewer blossoms, and has smooth leaves.
Habitat: Streambanks and gravelly slopes
Life Zone: Montane to alpine
Flowering Time: Summer to early fall

179

Wild Rose

(Woods' Rose)
Rosa woodsii
Rose Family - Rosaceae

This shrub can grow to 6 feet tall and has prickly stems and hooked spines at the base of each leaf. Flowers, up to 2 1/2 inches across, consist of 5 broad pink petals, with protruding yellow stamens and pistils. Leaves are compound and divided into 5 to 9 oval-shaped leaflets with toothed edges. Fruit (hard red rose hips) remains on the plant through winter and is rich in Vitamin C.

Habitat: *Valleys, gravelly soils, and along roadsides*
Life Zone: *Foothills to montane*
Flowering Time: *Late spring to summer*

White Elephantheads

Elephantheads
(Elephantella, Little Red Elephant)
Pedicularis groenlandica
Figwort Family - Scrophulariaceae
(APG III: Broomrape Family - Orobanchaceae)

Elephantheads are often found in large colonies in wet meadows and along streamsides. Plants can grow up to 2 feet tall and have a dense spike of pink to purple (rarely white) small flowers resembling upturned elephant's trunks. Leaves are fern-like and smaller toward the top of the plant. Stems are erect and purplish.
Habitat: Wet meadows and near streams
Life Zone: Montane to alpine
Flowering Time: Summer

181

Shooting Star

(American Cyclamen)

Dodecatheon pulchellum

Primrose Family - Primulaceae

Distinctive drooping flowers are on long, erect, fleshy stems up to 12 inches tall. Blossoms consist of pink to purple bent-back petals and a yellow base around a purplish point of fused stamens. Bright green leaves are long and elliptical and form a basal rosette. This plant is related to cyclamen.

Habitat: Damp meadows and streambanks

Life Zone: Foothills to subalpine

Flowering Time: Late spring to summer

Seed plumes

Prairie Smoke
(Old Man's Whiskers, Purple Avens)
Geum triflorum
(Syn: *Erythrocoma triflora*)
Rose Family - Rosaceae

Unique urn or bell-shaped blossoms, usually in groups of 3, nod or droop on reddish, hairy stems from 6 to 24 inches high. Dusky pink sepals and bracts enclose small petals. Mostly basal leaves are hairy and fern-like. Flowers turn skyward with age and form smoke-like puffs inspiring the common name for the plant.
Habitat: Mountain meadows and sagebrush habitats
Life Zone: Montane to subalpine
Flowering Time: Late spring to late summer

Dogbane (Trailing dogbane)
Apocynum androsaemifolium
Dogbane Family - Apocynaceae

Small white to pinkish bell-shaped flowers form in clusters on branching stems. Blossoms consist of 5 fused petals with reddish stripes on the inside. Bushy, branching plant grows from 8 to 20 inches tall and has drooping, shiny leaves. Leaves turn yellow-gold in late summer to fall. Stems are usually red and have a milky sap. Dogbane is considered toxic to humans and animals.

Habitat: Open hillsides, gravelly slopes, roadsides
Life Zone: Foothills to subalpine
Flowering Time: Summer to fall

Parry's Primrose
Primula parryi
Primrose Family - Primulaceae

Groups of bright, almost iridescent, pink flowers atop single stems are easily noticed. Plants are from 10 to 24 inches tall. Individual blossoms, 1 to 1 1/2 inches wide, have 5 petals surrounding a yellow center throat. Intense green leaves are basal and lance-shaped. If lightly touched, plants emit a putrid odor.
Habitat: Along streams, waterfalls, wet meadows
Life Zone: Montane to alpine
Flowering Time: Summer

Seed pods

Showy Milkweed
Asclepias speciosa
Milkweed Family - Asclepiadaceae
(APG III: Dogbane Family - Apocynaceae)

Round umbels of fragrant flowers grow on large, showy plants up to 6 feet tall. Individual flowers have 5 white to pink to purplish petals that are folded and bent back. Leaves are large, up to 12 inches, oblong, opposite and have reddish middle ribs. White and hairy seed pods are up to 4 inches long and covered with knobs. Hollow stems produce a milky sap.
Habitat: Ditch banks, roadsides, and fields
Life Zone: Plains to montane
Flowering Time: Summer

186

Narrowleaf Fireweed

Chamerion angustifolium (Syn: *Chamerion danielsii*)
Evening Primrose Family - Onagraceae

Fireweed, true to its name, is one of the first plants to grow and thrive after fire clears an area. It grows in colonies and reaches heights up to 5 feet tall. Bright pink flowers have 4 petals and form a spike with blossoms opening first at the bottom. Leaves are narrow and lance-shaped with a distinctive mid-vein. Seed pods are linear, purple, and release silky, hairy seeds.
Habitat: Dry places, along roadsides, and open fields
Life Zone: Montane to subalpine
Flowering Time: Summer

Hornemann's Willowherb
Epilobium hornemannii
Evening Primrose Family - Onagraceae

This slender plant can easily be overlooked with its tiny 4-petalled pink, white, or light blue flowers. It has an erect stem up to 15 inches tall topped with a few to many flowers that are upright to nodding. Leaves are oval to lance-shaped, up to 2 inches long, and often toothed or serrated. Stems and leaves often change to reddish colors in spring and fall.

Habitat: *Moist meadows, streamsides, and fields*
Life Zone: *Plains to subalpine*
Flowering Time: *Summer through beginning of fall*

Sticky Geranium

(Sticky Purple Crane's Bill)
Geranium viscosissimum
Geranium Family - Geraniaceae

Sticky Geranium grows to 3 feet tall and is often found in clumps. Hairs on the stems and sepals produce a sticky substance and a geranium odor. Fragrant and sticky flowers have 5 pink to lavender petals with dark red to purple veins. Mostly basal leaves are palmately divided and have toothed margins.

Habitat: Along roadsides, open woods, and meadows
Life Zone: Foothills to montane
Flowering Time: Late spring to summer

189

Lewis Monkeyflower (Purple Monkeyflower)
Mimulus lewisii
Figwort Family - Scrophulariaceae

(APG III: Lopseed Family - Phrymaceae)

Showy deep pink to red flowers consist of 2 upper and 3 lower lobes around throats with dark colored blotches and lines. Plants reach heights of 1 to 3 feet and have several stems with many wide, light-green lance-shaped leaves with toothed or plain edges. Flowers are grouped at tops of stems.
Habitat: Wet soils, along streams, wetland areas
Life Zone: Montane to subalpine
Flowering Time: Summer

Nodding Onion (Wild Onion)

Allium cernuum
Lily Family - Liliaceae
(APG III: Onion Family - Alliaceae)

Small pale pink or whitish flowers form in nodding clusters atop 6 to 20 inch stems. Basal leaves are grass-like with onion odor and taste. Flowers consist of 6 rounded tepals (petals and sepals are indistinguishable) and 6 yellow-tipped exserted stamens. Nodding Onion was a food source for early settlers and Native Americans.
Habitat: Open areas in woods, fields, and meadows
Life Zone: Foothills to subalpine
Flowering Time: Early to late summer

Twinberry Honeysuckle

(Bush Honeysuckle) *Lonicera involucrata*
(Synonym: *Distegia involucrata*)
Honeysuckle Family - Caprifoliaceae

This native, spreading shrub grows from 2 to 7 feet tall with grayish leafy stems. Tubular cream to yellow flowers form in pairs and are surrounded by broad red bracts. Bracts remain after the flowers to envelop two shiny black berries. Leaves are large, opposite and leathery with pointed tips.

Habitat: By mountain streams and on moist slopes
Life Zone: Foothills to subalpine
Flowering Time: Early summer to summer

Fairy-Slipper

(Calypso Orchid)
Calypso bulbosa
Orchid Family - Orchidaceae

This elegant native orchid grows in patches on short stems up to 5 inches high. Flower consists of 3 slender pink sepals, 2 small petals and one bulb-like petal that forms the slipper-shape, approximately 1 inch long with purple streaks. The endangered plant has a single basal leaf up to 2 1/2 inches long.
Habitat: In filtered light of conifer forests
Life Zone: Foothills to subalpine
Flowering Time: Spring to early summer

193

Scarlet Beeblossom (Scarlet Gaura)
Oenothera suffrutescens
(Synonym: *Gaura coccinea*)
Evening Primrose Family - Ornagraceae

Showy flowers appear at the end of arching stems that are from 6 to 12 inches tall. Flowers, 1/2 inch wide, range in colors from whites to pinks. Funnel-shaped blossoms consists of long tubes with 4 petals and pro-truding stamens and styles. Leaves are crowded along the stems and are hairy and grayish green.
Habitat: Roadsides, hillsides, and dry meadows
Life Zone: Foothills to montane
Flowering Time: Spring to summer

Gayfeather

(Dotted Blazing Star)
Liatris punctata
Sunflower Family - Asteraceae

Plants grow to 3 feet tall and have many stems with bright pinkish-purple flowerheads arranged in crowded spikes. Disk flowers twist around the stems and give the plant a feathery appearance. Leaves are alternate, linear, stiff, and have resin dots. Gayfeather is one of the last plants to bloom in summer.

Habitat: Shrubby area, roadsides, and sandy places
Life Zone: Foothills to montane
Flowering Time: Late summer to fall

195

Orange Hawkweed

Hieracium aurantiacum
Sunflower Family - Asteraceae

Orange hawkweed grows 10 to 20 inches tall and has oblong to spoon-shaped basal leaves with sometimes one or two small leaves along its bristly stem that has milky sap. Plants produce 5 to 35 hairy flowerheads. Red-orange strap-shaped ray flowers with notched tips surround a yellow-orange disk. This plant reproduces aggressively by runners crowding out native plants. It is on Colorado's List A of noxious weeds.

Habitat: *Moist grassy areas, meadows, along streams*
Life Zone: *Foothills to sub alpine*
Flowering Time: *Summer to fall*

Scarlet Globemallow (Copper Mallow)
Sphaeralcea coccinea)
Mallow Family - Malvaceae

Lovely orange-red flowers resembling miniature holly-hocks spread in patches and reach heights of 4 to 8 inches. Flowers are saucer-shaped with 5 broad round-ed petals with shallow notches. Leaves are alternate and palmately divided into 3 to 5 silver-gray green segments. Native Indians chewed roots and placed them on wounds to aid healing. Sweet-tasting teas were said to relieve upset stomachs and improve appetite.

Habitat: Roadsides, dry soils, open areas
Life Zone: Foothills to montane
Flowering Time: Spring to fall

Dame's Rocket
Hesperis matronalis
Mustard Family - Brassicaceae

This plant often appears in showy groupings. Pink to purplish 4-petaled flowers appear in elongated clusters atop long, hairy stems and leaves. Plants reach heights of 2 to 3 feet. Leaves are alternate, lance-shaped, toothed, and diminish in size toward the top of the stem. Dame's Rocket is on Colorado's noxious weed list B.

Habitat: Roadsides, disturbed soils
Life Zone: Foothills to montane
Flowering Time: Spring to summer

Water Smartweed (Water Knotweed)
Persicaria amphibia (Syn: *Polygonum amphibium*)
Buckwheat Family - Polygonaceae

Low-growing plants are terrestrial to aquatic and take root on land or at the edge of ponds or lakes. Stems can be erect or trail along the ground for up to 6 feet. Showy rose-pink flowers appear in a dense terminal cluster at the end of the long stems. Small individual flowers are cup-shaped with 5 parts and protruding stamens. Leaves are alternate and oval with pointed tips. Aquatic animals eat plant parts including the seeds.

Habitat: *Muddy areas, shallow water*
Life Zone: *Foothills to montane*
Flowering Time: *Summer to fall*

199

Pine Drops
Pterospora andromedea
Heath Family - Ericaceae

Pine Drops are parasitic plants living off fungi and stand among debris of conifer forest floors. Upright stems with spikes of bell-shaped flowers reach heights from 6 inches to over 3 feet. Pale yellow to pinkish flowers are clustered mainly at tops of plants and nod along its reddish-brown stems covered with fine hairs. Branchless stems become stiff with age.

Habitat: Conifer forests among organic debris
Life Zone: Foothills to montane
Flowering Time: Summer

Alpine Sorrel
Oxyria digyna
Buckwheat Family - Polygonaceae

Fleshy, long-lived plant grows from 2 to 14 inches tall usually on rock ledges or in rock crevices. Leaves up to 2 inches across are mostly basal and round or kidney-shaped and turn reddish in fall. Greenish to reddish flowers form a dense cluster up to 8 inches long and change to red to brown flat seeds at maturity. Leaves make a tasty addition to salads or sandwiches. Mountain Sorrel is rich in vitamins A, B, and C.

Habitat: *Meadows and rocky areas*
Life Zone: *Montane to alpine*
Flowering Time: *Summer to fall*

Kinnikinnick (Common Bearberry)
Arctostaphylos uva-ursi
Heath Family - Ericaceae

Ground cover shrub with woody stems grows low to the ground (4 to 8 inches high) and spreads in patches. Glossy dark green evergreen leaves are alternate and spoon-shaped with rounded tips. Bell-shaped pink to white flowers nod in small clusters at ends of branches. Bright red berries that are favorites of wildlife including bears form after the blossoms disappear. Long lasting berries are too tart and mealy for human tastes.
Habitat: *Open woods*
Life Zone: *Foothills to alpine*
Flowering Time: *Spring to summer*

202

Twinflower
Linnaea borealis
Honeysuckle Family - Caprifoliaceae

Delicate nodding pink to lavender flowers hang in pairs from thin, twin-forked stems. Funnel-shaped fragrant blossoms have 5 lobed fused petals and hairy throats. Low-growing evergreen plant reaches heights of 4 to 6 inches and its trailing stems form large patches. Leaves are rich green, alternate, small, round and have shallow teeth along upper edges. Plant was a favorite of Swedish scientist Carl Linnaeus, the father of modern botany.

Habitat: *Roadsides, dry soils, open areas*
Life Zone: *Montane to alpine*
Flowering Time: *Summer to fall*

203

Smallflower Sand Verbena

Tripterocalyx micranthus (Syn: *Abronia micrantha*)
Four O'Clock Family - Nyctaginaceae

Stems, leaves and flower tubes are covered with sticky, glandular hairs. Plants grow in sandy areas often with sand sticking to reddish-colored stems that trail along the ground but can be up to 24 inches tall. Flowers in small clusters consist of slender, greenish-red tubes opening into five small white divided lobes. Fruit has wide, net-veined or ribbed wings extending from capsule.

Habitat: Sandy areas, semi-desert, scrublands and gravelly roadsides
Life Zone: Foothills to montane
Flowering Time: Spring to fall

Pink Checkermallow
Sidalcea neomexicana
Mallow Family - Malvaceae

Tall lanky plants from 8 to 36 inches high are often hidden among other greenery in their environment, but their showy pink flowers with 5 petals and bundled stamens, stand out. Leaves are variable from upper leaves that are deeply divided and palmate to rounded basal leaves with toothed margins. Both leaves and stems are covered with white, silky hairs.

Habitat: Wet meadows, near streams and lakes
Life Zone: Montane
Flowering Time: Summer

Scurfpea (Slender-flowered Scurfpea)
Psoralidium tenuiflorum
(Syn: *Psoralea floribunda*)
Pea Family - Fabaceae

Small bluish to purple flowers grow in clusters on bushy, leafy plants up to 3 feet tall. Leaflets, 3 elongated, are all on short stalks. Oval-shaped seed pods end abruptly in a short beak. Plant stems are slender, wiry, branched, and upright to ascending. Scurfpea is a native plant and helps in adding nitrogen into the soil.
Habitat: Open woods, dry prairies, and rocky soils
Life Zone: Plains to foothills
Flowering Time: Late spring to fall

Slender Beardtongue (Lilac Penstemon)
Penstemon gracilis
Figwort Family - Scrophulariaceae

(APG III: Plantain Family - Plantaginaceae)

Slender, delicate plants reach heights of 8 to 24 inches tall. Flowers are arranged in loose spikes and grow on both sides of the stem. Lavender to purple blossoms are elongated tubes with 2 upper lips and 3 lower lips. Leaves have tiny teeth along the edges, are narrow tapering to a point, are attached opposite, and become progressively smaller toward the top of the stem.
Habitat: *Open woods, sandy and rocky soils*
Life Zone: *Plains to foothills*
Flowering Time: *Spring to early summer*

White Sky Pilot

Sky Pilot (Skunkweed)
Polemonium viscosum
Phlox Family - Polemoniaceae

Smelly funnel-shaped flowers form dense clusters on hairy, sticky stems up to 10 inches tall. Flowers have 5 blue to lavender lobes and hairy sepals. Basal leaves are pinnately divided into many small, sticky and hairy leaflets. Both the flowers and leaves of the plant can emit a "skunky" odor.

Habitat: Rocky slopes, disturbed meadows, along trails
Life Zone: Alpine
Flowering Time: Summer

Western Spiderwort (Prairie Spiderwort)
Tradescantia occidentalis
Spiderwort Family - Commelinaceae

Unique plant has intense blue flowers with 3 large petals and yellow-tipped anthers. Stems from 8 to 16 inches tall are topped with a cluster of up to 10 flowers. Leaves are long and grass-like, curling, and clasping the stems. "Spider" in the common name refers to the plant's leaves like spider legs, and the plant's stringy sap resembling a spider's web.

Habitat: Dry soils, sandy areas, meadows, along roads
Life Zone: Plains to foothills
Flowering Time: Summer

Flaxflowered Gilia

(Long-flowered Gilia)

Ipomopsis longiflora (Syn: *Gilia longiflora*)

Phlox Family - Polemoniaceae

This delicate plant has thin, wispy flowers and stems and grows up to 18 inches tall. Flowers range from pale blue, lavender, to white, and have very long, up to 3 inches, slender tubes that open out into 5 pointed lobes. Plants have many branches and stringy leaves that grow at intervals along the branches.

***Habitat:** Shrublands, open, sandy, semi-desert regions*

***Life Zone:** Foothills to montane*

***Flowering Time:** Spring to summer*

Rush Skeletonplant
Lygodesmia juncea
Sunflower Family - Asteraceae

Soft pink, bluish violet to white flowers have 5 ray flowers
with notches in tips and protruding stamens at the bases.
Bushy plants grow from 5 to 25 inches tall with clusters
of almost leafless rush-like stems. Stems can be upright
or along the ground and have prominent vertical grooves.
Leaves are short and linear and almost scale-like on the
upper stems.
Habitat: Sand, semi-desert, openings, and woodlands
Life Zone: Plains to foothills
Flowering Time: Summer to fall

211

Harebell

Parry's Harebell

Harebell

(Bell Flower, Bluebell of Scotland)
Campanula rotundifolia
Bellflower Family - Campanulaceae

This native perennial grows an average 12 inches tall and is found in small to large groupings. Nodding flowers are formed by 5 pointed petals fused together in a bell shape. Lavender to purple blossoms have Basal leaves are roundish and upper leaves are alternate and grass-like. Inset: Parry's Harebell, *Campanula Parryi*, has larger blossoms that face toward the sky.

Habitat: *Mountain slopes and meadows*
Life Zone: *Foothills to subalpine*
212 **Flowering Time:** *Summer to fall*

Upright Blue Beardtongue
Penstemon virgatus
Figwort Family - Scrophulariaceae

(APG III: Plantain Family - Plantaginaceae)

Spikes of pale violet to purple flowers grow on one side of tall stems to 18 inches high. Flowers consist of 2-lobed upper lips and 3-lobed lower lips and have dark purple streaks or guidelines inside. Beardtongue leaves are opposite, narrow, lanceolate, slightly folded, and have finely serrated edges. Leaves at the base of the plant are larger than those toward the top of the plant's stem.

Habitat: Roadsides, gravelly areas, and hillsides
Life Zone: Foothills to montane
Flowering Time: Summer

213

Pasqueflower

(Windflower, Easter Flower, Wild Crocus)
Pulsatilla patens   (Syn: *Pulsatilla ludoviciana*)
Buttercup Family - Ranunculaceae

Pasqueflowers are among the first wildflowers to bloom in springtime. Flowers, up to 2 inches across, have 5 to 7 lavender to purple sepals that are hairy outside and a paler color inside. Leaves are basal on stalks and divided into many narrow, pointed segments. All parts of the plant are poisonous and can irritate the skin.
Habitat: Open forests, meadows, and clearings
Life Zone: Montane to subalpine
Flowering Time: Spring to early summer

Blue Flax (Lewis' Flax, Wild Flax)
Linum lewisii   (Synonym: *Adenolinum lewisii*)
Flax Family - Linaceae

Open clusters of light to dark blue 5-petalled flowers grow on slender, branched stems up to 30 inches tall. Yellow centers consist of 5 stamens and 5 styles that are longer than the stamens. Flowers last for only one day, but the plants have many buds. Leaves are alternate and linear and cover the stem.
Habitat: Dry slopes, forest clearings, and roadsides
Life Zone: Foothills to subalpine
Flowering Time: Spring to summer

Tansy Aster
(Hoary Aster)
Dieteria canescens
(Syn: *Machaeranthera canescens*)
Sunflower Family - Asteraceae

Tall plants, 16 to 32 inches high, have many branching stems with 1 flowerhead per stem. Long-lasting bluish to purplish blossoms have narrow ray flowers around yellow disk flowers. Bracts have backward-curving tips. Leaves are narrow and toothed.
Habitat: *Roadsides, trails, and disturbed areas*
Life Zone: *Foothills to montane*
Flowering Time: *Summer to fall*

Alpine-Forget-Me-Not
Eritrichium nanum
(Synonym: *Eritrichum aretioides*)
Borage Family - Boraginaceae

Mat-forming plants grow to only 2 inches high and are often covered with masses of flowers. Tiny fragrant flowers form terminal clusters atop slender, hairy stems. Individual flowers are tubular, 1/4 inch across with 5 blue (sometimes white) lobes around a yellow throat. Leaves are basal, fleshy, and silvery in color with silky hairs along margins and tips.
Habitat: Open areas on ridges and rocky slopes
Life Zone: Subalpine to alpine
Flowering Time: Summer to late summer

217

Little Fringed Gentian
Gentianopsis barbellata
(Syn: *Gentiana barbellata*)
Gentian Family - Gentianaceae

This tiny plant has narrow fleshy leaves and a single stem topped with a blue to purple tubular flower. Lobes of the flower are quite variable and twisted with fringed edges. Plants grow from 2 to 6 inches high with a showy blossom up to 2 inches long. This gentian is not quite as common as the Fringed Gentian (page 219).
Habitat: *Grassy slopes and meadows*
Life Zone: *Montane to alpine*
Flowering Time: *Summer to early fall*

Fringed Gentian
Gentianopsis thermalis
(Syn: *Gentianopsis elegans*)
Gentian Family - Gentianaceae

These striking tubular flowers have 4 deep blue to purple lobes that are bent backwards with fringed edges. Flowers often appear in varying stages of twisting and striping and often unfold with the sun. Plants grow to 8 inches tall and have smooth erect stems. Upper leaves are opposite with up to 4 pairs per stem. Basal leaves are lanceolate to spatulate.
Habitat: Wet meadows, along streams, forest edges
Life Zone: Montane to subalpine
Flowering Time: Summer to early fall

Parry's Gentian

(Mountain Gentian, Bottle Gentian)
Gentiana parryi
(Synonym: *Pneumonanthe parryi*)
Gentian Family - Gentianaceae

Plants have stems from 9 to 16 inches tall with a terminal group of 1 to 6 blue to purple blossoms. Flowers have 5 fused petals like a barrel or bottle that split into 5 pointed main lobes with 5 smaller lobes or pleats between. Leaves are oval-shaped, sometimes pointed, smooth, and attached opposite along the stem.

Habitat: Meadows, streambanks and willow thickets
Life Zone: Montane to subalpine
Flowering Time: Summer to fall

Rocky Mountain Gentian
(Pleated Gentian)

Gentiana affinis   (Syn: *Pneumonanthe affinis*)
Gentian Family - Gentianaceae

Rocky Mountain Gentian grows from 4 to 20 inches tall and has many maroon-colored stems with long tubular flowers in tight unstalked clusters. Lower flowers have stalks. Unlike Parry's Gentian, this gentian may have flowers in leaf axils and blossoms are more cylindrical rather than barrel-shaped. Plants have numerous oval to lance-shaped leaves.

Habitat: In meadows, wooded areas, around streams
Life Zone: Montane to alpine
Flowering Time: Spring to summer

221

Lanceleaf Chiming Bells
Mertensia lanceolata
Borage Family - Boraginaceae

Many tiny, bell-shaped flowers, less than 1/2 inch long, cluster at the end of several stems that are 2 to 10 inches high. Unlike other bluebells, the anthers are enclosed within the flower tube and not visible with a casual glance. Leaves are lance-shaped, stalkless with stem being up to 15 inches long.

Habitat: Well-drained meadows and rock crevices
Life Zone: Subalpine to alpine
Flowering Time: Mid-summer to summer

Leafy Jacob's-Ladder
(Towering Jacob's-ladder)
Polemonium foliosissimum
Phlox Family - Polemoniaceae

Numerous showy clusters of sky blue to purple violet flowers are atop tall stems with ladder-like leaves. Plants grow from 2 to 4 feet tall and have an airy appearance. Flowers are a fused bell-shape with 5 lobes and stamens about the same length as the lobes. Like its cousin, Sky Pilot, Jacob's Ladder emits a "skunky" odor.
Habitat: *Meadows, open woods, and sunny hillsides*
Life Zone: *Montane to subalpine*
Flowering Time: *Summer to late summer*

Alfalfa
Medicago sativa
Pea Family - Fabaceae

This non-native plant grows to 3 feet tall with tight, rounded spikes of flowers on branched stems. It was originally introduced as a food crop for farm animals as it is high in protein and digestible fiber. Pea-like blossoms can range in color from pale blue to deep purple. Dark green leaves are in 3 parts like a clover, but are folded, narrow, and usually hairy.
Habitat: *Roadsides, in fields, and disturbed soils*
Life Zone: *Plains to foothills*
Flowering Time: *Spring to fall*

Chicory
Cichorium intybus
Sunflower Family - Asteraceae

Pale blue flowers up to 1 1/4 inches across are composed of square-tipped fringed petals. The plant with an unkempt appearance grows up to 4 feet high and has flowers sparsely spread on tall stems. Leaves are dandelion-like and mostly basal. Stem leaves are small and clasp the stem. Chicory is a non-native invasive plant and was once used as a coffee substitute.

Habitat: *Disturbed areas, roadsides, and fields*
Life Zone: *Plains to foothills*
Flowering Time: *Early summer to fall*

Lambert's Locoweed

(Purple Locoweed, Crazy Pea)
Oxytropis lambertii
Pea Family - Fabaceae

Flowers are spiked clusters of dark pinkish to purplish blossoms on leafless stems, 6 to 14 inches high. Lower petals or keels of flowers are pointed which distinguishes locoweed from milkvetches that have blunt or rounded keels. Leaves are compound and basal with lance-shaped leaflets. Hairy leaves give them a fuzzy, silvery appearance. Locoweeds are toxic to livestock.
Habitat: Grasslands and shrublands
Life Zone: Foothills to montane
Flowering Time: Late spring to summer

Showy Daisy
(Aspen or Purple Fleabane)
Erigeron speciosus
Sunflower Family - Asteraceae

Showy daisy is composed of numerous thin lavender ray flowers surrounding a yellow center of disk flowers. Plants have leafy stems from 7 to 30 inches high that branch near the top with each stalk supporting a single flower head, 1 1/2 to 2 inches wide. Leaves are long, lance-shaped, and smooth, often with 3 veins.
Habitat: Aspen groves, forest openings, and meadows
Life Zone: Foothills to subalpine
Flowering Time: Summer

227

Wild Iris
(Blue Flag)
Iris missouriensis
Iris Family - Iridaceae

This native perennial grows up to 2 feet high, usually in large, showy patches. Plants can sometimes cover whole fields transforming them to a sea of blue. Flowers are up to 4 inches across with 3 reflexed bluish-purple sepals with yellow-orange streaks, 3 erect petals, and 3 petal-like pistils. Basal leaves are long and sword-like. Roots and young sprouts are toxic.

Habitat: Moist open areas, meadows, and streamsides
Life Zone: Foothills to subalpine
Flowering Time: Late spring to summer

Colorado Columbine (Rocky Mountain Columbine)   *Aquilegia coerulea*
Buttercup Family - Ranunculaceae

Spectacular flower, up to 3 inches across, has 5 blue to lavender pointed sepals and 5 white scoop-shaped petals with slender blue spurs. Compound leaves are mostly basal on slim stalks and are dissected into sets of 3 rounded lobes. This protected species is a hermaphrodite, the blooms contain both male and female sex organs. The seeds and roots of the plant are very toxic. The Columbine is **Colorado's State Flower,** since it was designated by the State's general assembly in 1899.
Habitat: Open, moist forests, meadows, rocky slopes
Life Zone: Foothills to alpine
Flowering Time: Summer

229

Mat Penstemon
(Tufted Beardtongue)
Penstemon caespitosus
Figwort Family - Scrophulariaceae

(APG III: Plantain Family - Plantaginaceae)

This creeping or low-growing penstemon grows to only about 5 inches high but forms mats up to 3 feet in diameter. Flowers rise above the mat of leaves. Blossoms are bilateral with upper lobes flared and with lower lobes extending slightly longer than the upper. Colors are blue to purple. Small leaves are linear to spatulate.
Habitat: Dry, rocky disturbed slopes, woodlands
Life Zone: Foothills to montane
Flowering Time: Late spring to summer

Speedwell (Veronica)
Veronica wormskjoldii
(Synonym: *Veronica nutans*)
Figwort Family - Scrophulariaceae

(APG III: Plantain Family - Plantaginaceae)

Tiny blue flowers form a tight terminal cluster on hairy, erect stems up to 12 inches tall. Individual flowers consist of saucer-shaped flowers with 4 lobes, 4 hairy sepals, and 2 anthers. Leaves are opposite, oval-shaped and sometimes slightly toothed. Speedwell often grows in colonies with numerous plants. Leaves can be used for salad or for making herbal tea.

Habitat: *Wet areas and meadows*
Life Zone: *Montane to alpine*
Flowering Time: *Summer*

231

Blue Violet (Early Blue Violet)
Viola adunca
Violet Family - Violaceae

Tiny, single nodding flowers, up to 3/4 inch across, have 5 blue to purplish petals and 5 green to purple sepals. Base of the lowest petal has a sack-like spur. Plants form in clumps with slender, leafy stems up to 8 inches high. Leaves on stems are alternately attached and are oval to heart-shaped.
Habitat: In meadows, wooded areas, around streams
Life Zone: Montane to alpine
Flowering Time: Spring to summer

White Monkshood

Western Monkshood

Western Monkshood (Wolfbane)

Aconitum columbianum

Buttercup Family - Ranunculaceae

This native poisonous perennial can grow to heights of over 5 feet tall. Flowers at the top of the plant are on individual stems and consist of deep blue to purplish (white is rare) petal-like sepals which form a "hood" with a pointed beak over 2 lower sepals. Large leaves, up to 8" across, are palmately divided into 3-5 toothed lobes.

Habitat: Forest openings, moist soils, wet meadows
Life Zone: Montane to subalpine
Flowering Time: Summer

233

Tall Chiming Bells

Mertensia ciliata
Borage Family -
Boraginaceae

This plant can grow over 4 feet tall and has nodding clusters of light blue to pink bell-shaped flowers. Blue-green leaves are alternate, smooth and soft. They are edible as salad greens. This native variety often grows in clumps that can cover large areas.

Habitat: *Wet areas and along streams*
Life Zone: *Montane to alpine*
Flowering Time: *Summer*

Star Gentian
(Star Swerta, Felwort)
Swertia perennis
Gentian Family - Gentianaceae

Star-shaped flowers grow in small clusters atop slender stems up to 12 inches tall. Blossoms have 5 pointed blue-grey to purple and white petals, 5 narrow green sepals and protruding stamens. Leaves are mostly basal and spoon-shaped on long stalks.

Habitat: *Wet areas and meadows*
Life Zone: *Montane to subalpine*
Flowering Time: *Summer to fall*

Manyflower Stickseed

(False Forget-Me-Not)
Hackelia floribunda
Borage Family - Boraginaceae

Small pale blue flowers with yellow centers are arranged in dense clusters on stout, hairy stems from 1 to 4 feet tall. Blossoms with 5 petals are 1/4 of an inch across and droop with age. Leaves are narrow, lance-shaped and hairy underneath. Barb-tipped fruit nutlets cling to fur and clothing; hence the name Stickseed.

Habitat: Wet areas and meadows
Life Zone: Montane to subalpine
Flowering Time: Summer to fall

Silvery Lupine
Lupinus argenteus
Pea Family - Fabaceae

This common native plant has dense spiked clusters of pea-like flowers that vary in color from blue to purple and are sometimes bi-colored. Slender stems are 12 to 36 inches tall and have silvery-green leaves palmately divided into 5 to 9 narrow leaflets. Seedpods are flat and hairy. Silvery Lupine often creates large splashes of color in meadows.

Habitat: *Open woods, meadows, along roadsides*
Life Zone: *Foothills to subalpine*
Flowering Time: *Summer*

Narrowleaf Four-O'Clock

Mirabilis linearis
(Syn: *Oxybaphus linearis*)
Four-O'Clock Family - Nyctaginaceae

Small white, pink to red-purple flowers grow on a spindly plant up to 3 feet tall. Funnel shaped flowers, to 1/2 inch across, have 5 rounded, notched lobes and often coiled stamens. Bracts at the base of the blossoms are joined at the base and can be green or reddish color. Narrow leaves, stems and bracts are all covered with fine hairs.
Habitat: Dry sites, along trails, and roadsides
Life Zone: Plains to foothills
Flowering Time: Summer to early fall

Globe Gilia
Ipomopsis globularis
(Syn: *Ipomopsis spicata ssp. capitata*)
Phlox Family - Polemoniaceae

This rare plant is limited to the Mosquito Range and the Continental Divide in Park County. White to ice blue to pale lavender flowers form a dense, ball-like cluster atop a stout stem up to 6 inches tall. Flowers are quite fragrant and are often detected from many feet away before the plant is seen. Silky hairs around blossoms and stems give plants a woolly appearance.
Habitat: Rocky and gravelly soils
Life Zone: Alpine
Flowering Time: Summer to late summer

239

Gypsum Scorpionweed

White Scorpionweed

Scorpionweed (Gypsum Scorpionweed)

Phacelia integrifolia

Waterleaf Family - Hydrophyllaceae

(APG III: Borage Family - Boraginaceae)

This unique plant grows to 20 inches high and has a stout, hairy, sticky, stem. Flowers last for several weeks and are coiled at the end. Blue-lavender tubular blossoms are 1/4 inch wide with 5 rounded lobes and protruding purple stamens. Leaves are hairy and have scalloped edges. White Scorpion-weed, *Phacelia alba* has similar leaves.

Habitat: *Dry sandy and gravelly soils*
Life Zone: *Foothills to montane*
Flowering Time: *Spring to late summer*

Alpine Milkvetch (Alpine Astragalus)
Astragalus alpinus
Pea Family - Fabaceae

Plants form mats of leaves with many erect to prostrate stems from 1 to 10 inches high topped with short clusters of flowers. White to pink to purplish blue blossoms are 1/2 inch long and have dark, hairy sepals. Leaves, up to 6 inches long, are pinnately divided into 3/8 inch long leaflets. Seed pods are drooping and covered with fine black hairs.
Habitat: Meadows, open forests, and along streams
Life Zone: Montane to alpine
Flowering Time: Summer to late summer

241

Clustered Penstemon (Littleflower Penstemon)
Penstemon procerus
Figwort Family - Scrophulariaceae

(APG III: Plantain Family - Plantaginaceae)

Plants grow in patches with clusters of small flowers on stems up to 16 inches tall. Tubular flowers, 3/8 of an inch long, have 2-lobed upper lips and 3-lobed lower lips and range in color from light blue to bluish-purple. Stem leaves are narrow and clasping and basal leaves are lance-shaped and stalked.

Habitat: Meadows, open woods, and grassy slopes
Life Zone: Montane to alpine
Flowering Time: Summer to late summer

Dwarf Larkspur
Delphinium nuttallianun
(Syn: *Delphinium nelsonii*)
Buttercup Family - Ranunculaceae

This short plant, usually to 12 inches tall, has a cluster of dark blue to blue-purple flowers with spurs. Blossoms consist of 5 sepals to 3/4 of an inch long and 4 smaller petals. Top sepal has a long spur. Leaves are on long stalks and are deeply divided into palmate lobes.
Habitat: Meadows, open woods, and fields
Life Zone: Foothills to montane
Flowering Time: Early summer to summer

Subalpine Larkspur
Delphinium barbeyi
Buttercup Family - Ranunculaceae

Plants form several stems up to 6 feet tall from woody rootstocks. Showy fragrant flowers top stems in spike-like clusters. Blossoms consist of small petals and 5 deep blue to purplish sepals. Top sepal has a long spur. Large leaves are palmately divided in to 5 to 7 lobes with coarsely-toothed edges.

Habitat: Meadows, streambanks, and aspen woods
Life Zone: Subalpine
Flowering Time: Mid to late summer

Whipple's Penstemon

White Whipple's Penstemon

Whipple's Penstemon
Penstemon whippleanus
Figwort Family - Scrophulariaceae
(APG III: Plantain Family - Plantaginaceae)

Whipple's Penstemon ranges in color from deep burgundy to white with purple or bluish stripes. Clustered flowers are covered with tiny glandular hairs. Tubular blossoms have an upper lip and a bearded lower lip extending beyond it. Plants grow up to 20 inches tall or taller. Erect stems have lanceolate leaves.
Habitat: Moist meadows, streambanks, and bogs
Life Zone: Montane to alpine
Flowering Time: Early summer to fall

245

Rocky Mountain Penstemon
Penstemon strictus
Figwort Family - Scrophulariaceae

(APG III: Plantain Family - Plantaginaceae)

Rocky Mountain Penstemon is the tallest, up to 3 feet, of the species in the southern Rockies. Its color ranges from shades of pink, blue, and dark purple. Blossoms are mostly one-sided with extending anthers covered with long white hairs. Leaves are mostly lanceolate and upper leaves are often folded.

Habitat: *Woodlands, shrublands, and meadows*
Life Zone: *Foothills to montane*
Flowering Time: *Early to late summer*

Jacob's Ladder

Polemonium pulcherrimum ssp. delicatum
Phlox Family - Polemoniaceae

This showy plant grows to 10 inches tall with numerous slender woolly stems. Flowers, in small clusters, have 5 pale blue or violet petals and 5 green, pointed sepals. Leaves are alternate and pinnately divided into leaflets like a ladder. Groups of plants are often found under the shade of spruce trees.

Habitat: *In meadows, under conifers, along streams*
Life Zone: *Montane to subalpine*
Flowering Time: *Summer*

Purple Fringe (Silky Phacelia)
Phacelia sericea
Waterleaf Family - Hydrophyllaceae

(APG III: Borage Family - Boraginaceae)

Spiked clusters of purple flowers (3 to 7 inches) with protruding yellow-tipped stamens, grow on stout hairy stems up to 16 inches tall. Individual flowers, 1/4 of an inch long, are bell-shaped with hairy sepals. Leaves are deeply cut into silvery, hair lobes. Long stamens on the blooms look like pins in a pincushion. When touched, plants can cause skin irritations.

Habitat: Along trails, rocky soils, and forest openings
Life Zone: Subalpine to alpine
Flowering Time: Summer

Pale Blue-Eyed Grass

Blue-Eyed Grass

Pale Blue-Eyed Grass
Sisyrinchium pallidum
Iris Family - Iridaceae

Erect plant has grass-like leaves and grows from 4 to 16 inches tall. Pale blue flowers with darker blue veins are atop stiff, flattened stems. Flowers, approximately 1/2 inch across, have 6 pointed petals around a yellow center and open only in bright sunlight. Blue-Eyed Grass, *Sisyrinchium montanum,* is more common; it has darker blue-purple flowers and longer stems.

Habitat: *Open grasslands and meadows*
Life Zone: *Foothills to montane*
Flowering Time: *Summer to late summer*

Moss Gentian (Siberian Gentian, Pygmy Gentian)
Gentiana prostrata
(Syn: *Chondrophylla prostrata*)
Gentian Family - Gentianaceae

This tiny plant grows to 4 inches tall on either erect or prostrate slender, leafy stems. Tubular flowers, up to 1/2 inch across, consist of 4 to 5 lobes joined with pointed pleats. Flowers can be blue to blue violet. Smooth, oval-shaped leaves, less than 1/2 inch long, hug the stems.
Habitat: Grassy slopes, moist meadows, near ponds
Life Zone: Alpine
Flowering Time: Summer to late summer

Rock Clematis
Clematis Columbiana
(Synonym: *Atragene columbiana*)
Buttercup Family - Ranunculaceae

Slender, low-growing vine grows from 2 to 5 feet high on the open forest floor among rocks and ledges. Single bell-shaped flowers are soft violet blue to lavender blue and nod from a curved stem. Blossoms consist of 4 pointed petals up to 2 inches long. Leaves are cut into 2 or 3 parts with lobed or toothed edges.
Habitat: Open woods and in the shade of conifers
Life Zone: Foothills to montane
Flowering Time: Summer to fall

251

Weber's Saw-Wort
Saussurea weberi
Sunflower Family - Asteraceae

This rare plant was first seen in 1905 but not recognized as a separate species until 1959. It is a stout, unbranched plant that grows to 8 inches high. Rounded flowerhead is composed of stiff protruding disk flowers. Long, woolly lanceolate leaves surround the blossoms. Plant is limited mainly to Park and Summit Counties in Colorado and some areas of Wyoming and Montana.
Habitat: Grassy slopes, rocky soils
Life Zone: Alpine
Flowering Time: Summer to late summer

Britton's Skullcap
Scutellaria brittonii
Mint Family - Lamiaceae

Bluish-purple flowers are in pairs on 10 inch tall stems. Tubular blossom are 2-lipped and lower lip has white ribs. Leaves are opposite, to 2 inches long, hairy on top and smooth underneath. Stem is sticky, hairy, and usually branched at the base and is 4-sided or square like other mints. Dried leaves have been used by herbalists for over 250 years to treat nervous disorders.
Habitat: Open woods and in the shade of conifers
Life Zone: Foothills to montane
Flowering Time: Spring to summer

Hairy Daisy (Tall Fleabane)
Erigeron elatior
Sunflower Family - Asteraceae

This plant grows to 28 inches tall on leafy stems and often found in large clumps. Ray flowers, usually pink, can be blue violet or white. Center disk is yellow. Flowerheads, up to 1 inch across, have extremely woolly, hairy bracts. Buds are also fuzzy or hairy. Lance-shaped or triangular light green leaves and are clasping near the top of stem.
Habitat: *Moist and dry meadows*
Life Zone: *Montane to subalpine*
Flowering Time: *Summer to late summer*

Sugarbowl (Vase Flower, Leatherflower)
Clematis hirsutissima (Syn: *Coriflora hirsutissima*)
Buttercup Family - Ranunculaceae

Deep blue to purple flowers, up to 2 inches long, nod from single hairy stems from 12 to 24 inches tall. Unique blossom, resembling an upside down vase, consists of 4 leathery sepals. When flowers go to seed, they turn upright and form a feathery plume. Leaves are cut into narrow segments and have silvery hairs.
Habitat: Dry open areas and forest openings
Life Zone: Foothills to montane
Flowering Time: Spring to early summer

Ballhead Waterleaf

Hydrophyllium capitatum
Waterleaf Family - Hydrophyllaceae

(APG III: Borage Family - Boraginaceae)

Plants grow to approximately 1 foot tall with ball-shaped flowerheads appearing beneath the leaves. Dense bluish-purple flower clusters are composed of bell-shaped flowers with 5 petals, 5 sepals with stiff hairs, and 5 exserted stamens. Leaves on long stalks are divided into 5 to 7 leaflets with 2 to 3 pointed lobes.
Habitat: Moist soils, wooded and open areas
Life Zone: Montane to subalpine
Flowering Time: Spring to summer

Bluemist Penstemon (Bluemist Beardtongue)
Penstemon virens
Figwort Family - Scrophulariaceae
(APG III: Plantain Family - Plantaginaceae)

Plants with many hairy stems grow in clusters to up to 15 inches tall. Blue flowers are arranged in separated groupings along the stems. Basal leaves are light green and shiny and smaller upper leaves clasp the stem. Blossoms have 2 upper lips and 3 wider lower lips around a broad, open throat. This plant is more common on the eastern slopes of Wyoming and Colorado.
Habitat: Rocky, gravelly areas
Life Zone: Foothills to montane
Flowering Time: Summer to late summer

257

Western Sweet Cicely (Sweet Cicely)
Osmorhiza occidentalis
Parsley Family - Apiaceae

Sweet Cicely smells like anise or licorice. Root, leaves, and seeds of the plant are all aromatic and edible. Plants grow from 2 to 4 feet tall with umbels of tiny inconspicuous green to white flowers that are more noticeable when they go to seed. Leaves have toothed margins and are pinnately divided on stalks.

Habitat: In meadows, shrublands, woodlands
Life Zone: Montane to subalpine
Flowering Time: Summer

Green Gentian (Monument Plant, Elkweed)
Frasera speciosa　　(Syn: *Swertia radiata*)
Gentian Family - Gentianaceae

This plant may show only as an upright basal rosette of leaves for many years until a monumental flower stalk to 6 feet tall or more appears. Flowers are white to greenish with 4 to 5 petals joined at the base and are clustered along a stout, unbranched stem. Blossoms have purple glands and dots and hairs inside. Narrow lance-shaped leaves whorl around the stem.
Habitat: *Pine forests, meadows, and along roadsides*
Life Zone: *Montane to alpine*
Flowering Time: *Summer*

259

Narrowleaf Burreed
Sparganium angustifolium
Burreed Family - Sparganiaceae

These aquatic plants have floating stems to 20 inches tall and leaves that are partially above water. Burreed flowers are dense sphere-shaped heads of male flowers along upper parts of the stem and female flowerheads near the base of the stem. Leaves are long and narrow and curled and appear rounded on the backs.

Habitat: Marshy meadows and ponds
Life Zone: Montane
Flowering Time: Summer

Snow-on-the-Mountain
Euphorbia marginata
Spurge Family - Euphorbiaceae

Clusters of small, inconspicuous flowers with white petals are surrounded by showy leaves with white margins. Plants grow from 1 to 2 feet tall and have a single stem that branches to form a flat or umbrella-shaped top. Snow-on-the-Mountain produces a milky sap that can cause skin irritations.

Habitat: Dry hillsides and roadsides
Life Zone: Foothills
Flowering Time: Spring to fall

One-sided Wintergreen (One-sided Pyrola)
Orthilia secunda   (Syn: *Pyrola secunda*)
Wintergreen Family - Pyrolaceae

(APG: Heath Family - Ericaceae)

Tiny greenish-white flowers hang from one side of a bent stem. Individual blossoms, up to 1/4 inch long, consist of 5 cup-shaped petals with a protruding style. Deep green leaves are evergreen, giving the plant its common name, "wintergreen". Oval to round, fleshy leaves are alternate and group around the lower part of the plant. The flower is often found near spruce trees.

Habitat: *Moist, shady spots in willows and forests*
Life Zone: *Montane to subalpine*
Flowering Time: *Summer*

Fringed Sage (Silver Sage, Pasture Sage)
Artemisia frigida
Sunflower Family - Asteraceae

Silvery gray-green, finely cut foliage is topped with long, hairy and leafy stems with numerous flowerheads. The flowerheads form spike-like clusters of nodding tiny white to yellow disk flowers. Plants grow in tufts from 4 to 16 inches tall and have the familiar sage aroma. Leaves are alternately arranged along the plant stems. This native herb is quite common throughout Colorado.

Habitat: *Dry meadows, gravelly slopes and shrublands*
Life Zone: *Foothills to montane*
Flowering *Time: Summer to fall*

Western Coneflower (Rayless Coneflower)
Rudbeckia occidentalis
Sunflower Family - Asteraceae

Flowerheads are dark brown to purplish egg to cone-shaped heads composed only of disk flowers. Large leaves are alternately attached and usually oval but pointed and have light to deeply toothed edges. These striking native plants grow from 3 1/2 to 6 feet tall and are found mostly in Western Colorado as well as Utah, Wyoming and north to Western Montana.

Habitat: Moist meadows or lightly wooded areas
Life Zone: Foothills to montane
Flowering Time: Summer to early fall

Giant Angelica

Gray's Angelica

Giant Angelica
Angelica ampla
Parsley Family - Apiaceae

Plant produces a large umbrella-shaped flowerhead atop a stout stalk growing to over 3 feet tall. Leaves are compound, alternate and divided into toothed leaflets. New leaf stems are surrounded by buff to maroon colored sheaths clasping the stem. Gray's Angelica, *Angelica grayi*, is much smaller, 6 to 24 inches tall, and appears above treeline on dry rocky slopes. Angelica plants have therapeutic properties.

Habitat: *Mountain streamsides and moist meadows*
Life Zone: *Montane to alpine*
Flowering Time: *Summer to early fall*

White to Cream Wildflowers by Common Name

White to Cream Wildflowers by Common Name

Claret Cup Cactus, *Echinocereus triglochidiatus*, also called King Cup Cactus, became the **official State Cactus of Colorado** in March 2014.

Yellow to Orange Wildflowers by Common Name

Red to Pink Wildflowers by Common Name

Blue to Purple Wildflowers by Common Name

Green Wildflowers by Common Name

The Author

Linda Nagy, born in Georgia, has a BFA and MFA in graphic design. She has always been passionate about flowers, especially wildflowers. When she retired to Colorado with her husband in 2003, she began studying and identifying native plants growing in the nearby Mountain Ranges. Linda is a member of the Colorado Native Plant Society and has earned her Colorado Flora Certificate. She is also a watercolor artist and free-lance writer for several local and regional newspapers and magazines.

The Photographer

Bernie Nagy, born in Austria, studied graphic arts, printing and photography. He worked throughout Europe and the Middle East as a offset technician, photo journalist, and travel writer before immigrating to the States in 1967. He and his wife owned a direct marketing/ mail order business for 33 years before they retired and moved from Georgia to South Park, Colorado in 2003. Falling in love with the local history and mountains, Bernie contributed for many years articles and photographs to Colorado publications and magazines & published award winning coffee table photo books to showcase Colorado's South Park and Park County's History. Since 2010 the artist couple ventured through high mountain meadows and along hiking trails in the Rocky Mountains to capture all the images of wildflowers for this special guide book.

References for Further Study

BOOKS:

Anthony, Steve, Tim D'Amato and others, *Noxious Weeds of Colorado*. Ninth Addition. Colorado: Colorado Weed Management Association. 2007.

Darrow, Katherine, *Wild about Wildflowers: Extreme Botanizing in Crested Butte, Wildflower Capital of Colorado*. Colorado: WildKat Publishing, 2006.

Guennel, G. K., *Guide to Colorado Wildflowers Volume 1: Plains & Foothills, Vol. 2: The Mountains*. Colorado: Westcliffe Publishers, 1995.

Pesman, M. Walter and Dan Johnson, *Meet the Natives: A Field Guide to Rocky Mountain Wildflowers, Trees, and Shrubs: Bridging the Gap Between Trail and Garden*. 11th Edition. Big Earth Publishing Co., 2012.

Schneider, Al, Lewis, and Whitney Tilt, *Colorado Rocky Mountain Wildflowers:* High Country Apps, LLC, 2012.

Spellenberg, Richard, *National Audubon Society Field Guide to North American Wildflowers Western Region*. Second Edition. New York: Canticleer Press, Inc. 2010.

Weber, William A. and Ronald C. Whitmann. *Colorado Flora Western Slope: A Field Guide to the Vascular Plants*. Fourth Edition. Colorado: University Press Colorado, 2012.

Weber, William A., *Rocky Mountain Flora*. Fifth Edition. Colorado: University Press of Colorado, 1976.

WEBSITES FOR WILDFLOWERS:

http://www.bonap.org

http://www.coloradowildflowers.org

http://www.denverplants.com/wflwr/index.htm

http://jeffco.us/coopext/intro.jsp

http://plants.usda.gov

http://www.swcoloradowildflowers.com

http://www.wildflowersofcolorado.com/